THE FUNAMBULIS
VOLUME 09

CW01429454

SCIENCE FICTION

Edited by Léopold Lambert
May 2014

THE FUNAMBULIST PAMPHLETS
VOLUME 09: SCIENCE FICTION
© **Léopold Lambert, 2014.**

http://creativecommons.org/licenses/by-nc-nd/3.0/

This work is Open Access, which means that you are free to copy, distribute, display, and perform the work as long as you clearly attribute the work to the authors, that you do not use this work for commercial gain in any form whatsoever, and that you in no way alter, transform, or build upon the work outside of its normal use in academic scholarship without express permission of the author and the publisher of this volume. For any reuse or distribution, you must make clear to others the license terms of this work.

First published in 2014 by
The Funambulist + CTM Documents Initiative
an imprint of punctum books
Brooklyn, New York
http://punctumbooks.com

ISBN-13: 978-0692226803
ISBN-10: 069222680X

Cover by the author (2014)

Acknowledgements to Eileen Joy, Anna Kłosowska, Ed Keller, Martin Byrne, Marc-Antoine Mathieu, Iker Gil, and Koldo Lus Arana.

INDEX

INTRO

WHEN JAMES GRAHAM BALLARD MEETS PHILIP K. DICK, WHAT DO THEY TALK ABOUT?

The following texts are not all addressing what should be considered as science fiction per se. Can James Graham Ballard's masterpiece *Crash* (1973) be called science fiction? Probably not in the sense of Jules Verne, Isaac Asimov and Stanislaw Lem. On the other hand, Ballard questions the way technology affects our bodies and how a creative sexuality can emerge from this relationship seems to me fundamentally a science fiction type of problem. Having James Graham Ballard and Philip K. Dick as the two protagonists of the following texts constitutes an indirect way to reflect on architecture as a technology. Juxtaposing these two authors creates a dialogue that may be as relevant as the most rigorous theoretical work dedicated to these questions. Ballard is fascinated by the beauty and sometimes the eroticism provoked by the failure of technology; Dick is wondering how much human we might remain when our own body is a technological product. Ballard and Dick are not, however, the only 'characters' of these texts in which many more political, philosophical and mythological arguments are being made through the often underrated medium of science fiction.

01

SCIENCE FICTION AS AN INVENTOR OF DILEMMAS: *FROM UTOPIA TO APOCALYPSE* BY PETER PAIK

The subject of this chapter is directly inspired by the reading of *From Utopia to Apocalypse: Science-Fiction and the Politics of Catastrophe* (University of Minnesota Press, 2010) by Peter Y. Paik. Science Fiction proposes dilemmas that should not be considered less problematic and important than Greek Mythology. One could even argue that these dilemmas are more crucial. In fact, the Greeks were introducing problems concerning nation and family (Antigone, Orestes), the dilemmas proposed by certain works of science fiction involve modes of existence. With the Holocaust, the 20th century invented the administrative genocide involving a narrative of responsibility delegated to the direct superior hierarchical representative. As Hannah Arendt showed, the Holocaust was only possible because of the participation of every single cog of the administration implementing it.

In order to introduce such problems, Paik chose five literary and cinematographic works that belong to the realm of science-fiction:

- The comic book *Watchmen* by Alan Moore & Dave Gibbons (1987)

- The film *Save the Green Planet* by Jang Joon-Hwan (2003)
- The manga *Nausicaa of the Valley of Wind* by Hayao Miyazaki (1982)
- The film *The Matrix* by Andi & Lana Wachowski (1999)
- The comic book *V for Vendetta* by Alan Moore (1982-1989)

Save the Green Planet dramatizes the systematic and inhumane torture of several individuals by the main character who wants to save the planet from an alien invasion, thus introducing the question of the end that justifies the means.

Nausicaa of the Valley of Wind questions the problem of violence as a form of resistance through its main character who is resolute to solve conflicts without it.

The Matrix wonders if freedom and truth are more important than happiness by imagining a "real" world beyond the one we experience on a daily basis that would be nothing else than illusory signals in our brains.

The two comic books, *Watchmen* and *V for Vendetta* created by Alan Moore propose particularly difficult dilemmas:

Watchmen narrates the action of several characters whose respective personalities dictate their actions and choices. Three of them in particular construct the main dilemma of the book: the Comedian, who is presented as a brute who pathologically rapes and murders innocent people, Rorschack, a dark and solitary vigilante who lives only for principles, and Ozymandias who appears at first sight as handsome, successful, infinitely rich and full of good intentions but is later understood as a merciless pragmatic.

The story starts with the mysterious murder of the Comedian — his life is depicted through flashbacks all along the book — and finishes by a conversation between Rorschack and Ozymandias after the latter sent a monstrous creature destroying New York City and its population. The calculated effect of this massive remote murder is to bring USA and the Soviet Union to cancel their nuclear attacks and unite in universal peace. Ozymandias is therefore the character who brings world peace by killing several thousands people, and Rorschack the one who, by his principles that make him condemn this choice is an abstract symbol (he wears a mask), dehumanized and unable to reach any form of solidarity. The Comedian, despite his cruelty, appears therefore as the most ambiguous and thus human of these three character as he counts himself fully responsible for his acts and their effects.

V for Vendetta tackles a similar problem. Its main character, V, a masked resistant to totalitarianism, has a personality and principles that, just like Rorschack's, bring him to a level of dehumanization that transforms him into a disincarnated symbol. This status is particularly observable when he kidnaps Evey (the second main character, who realizes little by little the totalitarian system in which she lives) and pretends, for several weeks to be part of the secret services by torturing and interrogating her to the point of her mocked execution. When she still remains silent, she is set free from all fear and according to V, she reaches real freedom. She is thus liberated by a man who conscientiously imprisoned and tortured her in the name of freedom.

Like any real problems, the ones introduced here do not have a "right solution." Beyond the difficulty of choosing one option or another in any given dilemma, what is really important is whether the person making this choice holds her/himself responsible for such choice. The idea behind Paik's book is to point out such problems of choice and responsibility within the context of narrative works that have been universally received and can be transposed to choices closer to the ones we have to make on a daily basis.

Originally published on February 26, 2011

02

2037 BY RAJA SHEHADEH

[also in The Funambulist Pamphlets Volume 6: PALESTINE]

Raja Shehadeh is a Palestinian lawyer who lives in Ramallah and has devoted his whole carreer to issues concerning Palestinian land expropriated by Israeli colonizing power. I met him in July 2010 in Ramallah for an interview about the practice of law as a resistance against the Israeli occupation of the West Bank and East Jerusalem. Back then, his book Palestinian Walks: Forays into a Vanishing Landscape had just been translated and published in France by Galaade and his book A Rift In Time: Travels With My Ottoman Uncle was being released by Profile Books. He now publishes (only in French, as much as I know) a new short beautiful book, 2037 Le Grand Bouleversement (Galaade, 2011), a sort of fictitious manifesto.

2037 is divided in two parts. The first is another version of history than the one we usually receive in the Western world. This version does not deny the suffering of the Jewish people, reaching the ultimate horror in the Holocaust. However, it tells the story of the Palestinians from the beginning of the 20th century who little by little lost power of their country so that eventually their land was occupied by a foreign army. The second part gave the book its name. 2037 is the year when the scene described by Raja in his book occurs. "Le Grand Bouleversement" (The Great Upheaval) is a fictitious earthquake that triggers a nuclear accident, reestablishing solidarity between Arab Countries, Palestinians and Israelis. The scene takes place in 2037, when radiation has decreased enough to allow the Middle East to work in a similar way as the European Union is currently working. Shehadeh evokes trains between Istanbul, Damascus, Jerusalem and Jericho that go every 30 minutes, some Israelis and Palestinians gathering as friends and cultural and sports events in a new land, liberated from barbed wires and other border apparatuses. Nevertheless, Shehadeh is not establishing a naive dream of a world uniting at the "end of history." On the contrary, he makes sure to draw the reader's attention to new issues that would occur in such a world, that is, a paradoxical religious antagonism against anything that has to do with religion, to the point of fanaticism and that appears redundant and inevitable in human history. By tackling these new issues, he succeeds in making us forget that the future world he describes is actually far from the current situation. As he points out in the first part, the economic and political class of the Israeli State depends so much on the apartheid establishment against Palestinians, it seems more likely to imagine a deus ex machina provoking an earthquake rather than a sudden action on behalf the international community and even less Israel itself.

.....

Originally published on June 2, 2011

03

COLLISION, SEXUALITY AND RESISTANCE

[also in The Funambulist Pamphlets Volume 4: LEGAL THEORY]

COLLISION, SEXUALITY AND RESISTANCE ///
(originally written for the 2012 Melbourne Doctoral Forum on Legal Theory "Law and its Accidents")

Calling for papers about law and its accident is indubitably recognizing that law is a technology, and that each technology implies the invention of its own failure, as Paul Virilio points out. Accident could be defined as the moment when technology ceases to function after its collision with another body. The violence of such collision is normally understood as unfortunate, if not fatal.

In 1973, the English author James Graham Ballard published *Crash*, a novel that extensively describes a new form of sexuality reaching its climax at the very moment of the accident. He uses the car as the paradigm of modern technocracy and introduces his characters as the pioneers of this sexuality. Each scar is a trace of a previous accident, and becomes a new orifice that constructs these characters' desire until the next machinist orgasm. The orgasm is produced by the sudden penetration of the piece of technology into the human body. This event celebrates the death of technology and often implies the death of the human body that depende on it.

This brief exposé of Ballard's novel does not immediately call forth an analogy to law, but if we reconsider the accident as defined above, we can think of the various national revolutions throughout history — including the most recent ones in the Arab world — as a collision of the law with another body — the people — before its complete suspension that marks the end of a regime.

Revolution is based on the production of a desire that ultimately effectuates itself through a punctual and jubilatory event that we can metaphorically envision as a collective orgasm. Just like in *Crash*, technology does not 'die' without the violence of the collision, and the various suppressions that we observed in the Arab world are symptomatic of such violence. In Iran, for example, this suppression implied the law to its highest degree: organizing trials and condemning numerous activists of the Green Revolution to death. Various emergency laws adopted in several countries also carry this violence, as they suspend the law within the very frame of the legal system.

Just as sexuality, a revolution should not be characterized by its finality, what we called here the accident. Rather, it should be characterized by the continuous production of desire that precedes this event. During the recent Egyptian revolution, the intensive moment was not as much Husni Mubarak's termination as the eighteen days spent by the protesters on Tahrir Square in Cairo. These three weeks constituted the desire for democracy within its own production at the scale of a micro-society.

Gilles Deleuze and Félix Guattari are fundamental to understand this mechanism as they define the body as a productive machine of desire (see The Funambulist Pamphlets Volume 03: Deleuze), while defining machine as the martial formation of devenir révolutionnaire (revolutionary becoming). This devenir révolutionnaire has a name: resistance.

.....

Originally published on January 28, 2012

04

BALLARDIAN LANDSCAPES: DESACRALIZING THAUMATURGIC MODERNITY

I would like to speak about breakage, crisis, dysfunction what we usually call failure. We find failure as a generative element in many narratives. We can think of the fly in Terry Gilliam's *Brazil* (1985), whose little corpse falls into the administrative machine, creates a typo in the registers and eventually orders the arrest of an honest citizen that triggers the entire plot of the film. Similarly, there cannot be *Heart of Darkness* (Joseph Conrad, 1899) without Kurtz's madness, nor can there be an *Animal Farm* (George Orwell, 1945) without the death of the Old Major pig.

James Graham Ballard's literary work is entirely built upon this notion of failure. In his case, it is the failure of modernism's promises and of a thaumaturgic and messianic technocracy. Let's consider the novella *The Thousand Dreams of Stellavista* (1962) as a paradigm of this literary construction: the narrator moves in a "psychotropic" house that morphologically responds to the state of mind of its inhabitant at any given moment. It is a literal incarnation of the vision of the smart city as progressist imaginaries were constructing it in the 1960s. Ballard subverts this dream of ubiquitous comfort and describes for us the traumatic neuroses that this house experiences after having hosted the murder of its previous inhabitant. These psychological troubles will culminate in the attempt to assassinate the narrator:

> 'Howard, this house is insane, I think it's trying to kill me!' […]
> Then, abruptly, the room stilled. A second later, as I lifted myself up on one elbow, a violent spasm convulsed the room, buckling the walls and lifting the bed off the floor. The entire house started to shake and writhe. Gripped by this seizure, the bedroom contracted and expanded like the chamber of a dying heart, the ceiling rising and falling. (James Graham Ballard, "The Thousand Dreams of Stellavista," in *Vermillon Sands,* Berkeley Books, 1971.)

This literal failure can be found more broadly in the entirety of Ballard's work: the skyscraper of *High Rise* (1975) where social hierarchy corresponds to its verticality and that ends in a revolutionary chaos. *Concrete Island* (1974) is a modern rewriting of Robinson Crusoe where the desert island cut off from all contact with society is an area between three highway ramps. In *Running Wild* (1988), modern and comfortable gated community's children massacre their parents. Londoner middle class transforms into violent and nihilist insurgents in *Millenium People* (2003). Ballard does not play with his readers, he develops a true esthetics of failure.

Ballardian landscapes have the same colors as Michelangelo Antonioni's *Red Desert* (1964): grey is ubiquitous in an atmosphere that seems to be the product of factories and cars that populate these landscapes. Only the televisual colors remain bright when they show us the faces of Ronald Reagan and Margaret Thatcher. Ballard takes care to desacralize these idols, to soil them with their corporal matter.

Ballard's masterpiece, *Crash* (1973) is the proof that he is not amused by failure, but rather considers it in its potential constructivism. In this novel, Ballard imagines a new sexuality that crashed bodies develop with their car during the crash itself. The penetration of car components in the driver's body thus composes an aristophanic body (two bodies that attempt to form a unique one) between the human and technology.

Still from *Crash* by David Cronenberg (1996)

Vaughan unfolded for me all his obsessions with the mysterious eroticism of wounds, the perverse logic of blood-soaked instrument panels; seat-belts smeared with excrement, sunvisors lined with brain tissue. For Vaughan, each crashed car set off a tremor of excitements in the complex geometries of a dented fender, in the unexpected variations of crushed radiator grilles, in the grotesque overhang of an instrument panel forced onto a driver's crotch as if in some some calibrated act of machine fellation. (James Graham Ballard, *Crash*, Jonathan Cape Publisher, 1973)

This sexuality that embraces desacralized modernity — or maybe its pagan sacrality in Antonin Artaud's way — constitutes a way to built on modernity's ruins. This construction is more ambiguous but also less moralizing and less dependent on the modern thaumaturgic dreams as Ballard's poetic manifesto *What I Believe* indicates:

> I believe in the light cast by video-recorders in department store windows, in the messianic insights of the radiator grilles of showroom automobiles, in the elegance of the oil stains on the engine nacelles of 747s parked on airport tarmacs. (James Graham Ballard, "What I Believe." in *Interzone, #8*, Summer 1984.)

.....

Originally published on May 24, 2014

05

THE FOULED BEAUTY OF
JAMES GRAHAM BALLARD

The poem that I included at the end of this chapter could be said to constitute James Graham Ballard's manifesto, as its title, "What I believe," indicates. The repetition of "I believe" at the beginning of each sentence of this poem reinforces this hypothesis; however, its contents also consist in the construction of an aesthetics that can be found in Ballard's literary work. It is important to stress the fact that this is in no way a counter-aesthetics that would be composed of all antipodes from the dominant ideal. This is not a beauty carved in the negative of another but veritably a positive construction for what is fouled, what triggers an ambiguity between disgust and fascination. Such an aesthetic has been so strongly carried within his work that it created an interpretation of the world that can be called by the adjective neologism, *ballardian*, just as the world created by one of Ballard's heroes, Franz Kafka, is called kafkaesque.

While Andy Warhol dehumanizes an actress by making an icon out of her, James Graham Ballard considers an iconic figure of the United Kingdom's 1980s politics, Margaret Thatcher, and brings her back to what she really is: a body with its genital organs, its postures and its smells. In doing so, he accomplishes a true political act. What I mean by that is that insisting on her body, as well as Ronald Reagan's, and their non-glamorous characteristics should not be considered a form of political satire, but rather demystification of the spectacular (in the "Debordian" sense) myths that built these political personalities.

Just like Antonin Artaud did in his work, Ballard is fascinated by organs that externalize the internal production of the body. Mouths and "sweet odours emanating from their lips", the ass and its excrement that "smears the seat belts" in crashed automobiles, and, of course, the genital organs and their ejaculative matter. However, Artaud "re-injects" some transcendence into this matter as he inscribes it within the practice of rituals from a sort of pagan religion. On the contrary, in *Crash* (Jonathan Cape Publisher, 1973), Ballard celebrates the beauty of sperm and gush through the very pagan event of the accident that he sees as the mechanical production of new orifices from which the various liquids and smells of the machine are ejected. The accident couples machines with machines (and in the book, oftentimes, humans with humans), but also machines with humans, the body of each penetrating the other in a de-gendered coitus.

We can interpret this as an allegory of the relationship between humans and machines, as in Antoine Picon's in *La ville territoire des cyborgs* (The city as a territory of cyborgs) (Editions de l'Imprimeur, 1998), but what this poem reveals is something more present, more literal in Ballard's interest: the fouled beauty of bodies, machines and places and the slow or accelerated decay that acts upon them. If he sees beauty in it, it is probably because of the vertigo for its irremediability and the unpredictability of its physical production.

>>>

WHAT I BELIEVE ///
By James Graham Ballard in *Interzone, #8*, Summer 1984. A prose poem, originally published in French in *Science Fiction #1* (ed. Daniel Riche) in January 1984.

I believe in the power of the imagination to remake the world, to release the truth within us, to hold back the night, to transcend death, to charm motorways, to ingratiate ourselves with birds, to enlist the confidences of madmen.

I believe in my own obsessions, in the beauty of the car crash, in the peace of the submerged forest, in the excitements of the deserted holiday beach, in the elegance of automobile graveyards, in the mystery of multi-storey car parks, in the poetry of abandoned hotels.

I believe in the forgotten runways of Wake Island, pointing towards the Pacifics of our imaginations.

I believe in the mysterious beauty of Margaret Thatcher, in the arch of her nostrils and the sheen on her lower lip; in the melancholy of wounded Argentine conscripts; in the haunted smiles of filling station personnel; in my dream of Margaret Thatcher caressed by that young Argentine soldier in a forgotten motel watched by a tubercular filling station attendant.

I believe in the beauty of all women, in the treachery of their imaginations, so close to my heart; in the junction of their disenchanted bodies with the enchanted chromium rails of supermarket counters; in their warm tolerance of my perversions.

I believe in the death of tomorrow, in the exhaustion of time, in our search for a new time within the smiles of auto-route waitresses and the tired eyes of air-traffic controllers at out-of-season airports.

I believe in the genital organs of great men and women, in the body postures of Ronald Reagan, Margaret Thatcher and Princess Di, in the sweet odors emanating from their lips as they regard the cameras of the entire world.

I believe in madness, in the truth of the inexplicable, in the common sense of stones, in the lunacy of flowers, in the disease stored up for the human race by the Apollo astronauts.

I believe in nothing.

I believe in Max Ernst, Delvaux, Dali, Titian, Goya, Leonardo, Vermeer, Chirico, Magritte, Redon, Dürer, Tanguy, the Facteur Cheval, the Watts Towers, Boecklin, Francis Bacon, and all the invisible artists within the psychiatric institutions of the planet.

I believe in the impossibility of existence, in the humour of mountains, in the absurdity of electromagnetism, in the farce of geometry, in the cruelty of arithmetic, in the murderous intent of logic.

I believe in adolescent women, in their corruption by their own leg stances, in the purity of their disheveled bodies, in the traces of their pudenda left in the bathrooms of shabby motels.

I believe in flight, in the beauty of the wing, and in the beauty of everything that has ever flown, in the stone thrown by a small child that carries with it the wisdom of statesmen and midwives.

I believe in the gentleness of the surgeon's knife, in the limitless geometry of the cinema screen, in the hidden universe within supermarkets, in the loneliness of the sun, in the garrulousness of planets, in the repetitiveness or ourselves, in the inexistence of the universe and the boredom of the atom.

I believe in the light cast by video-recorders in department store windows, in the messianic insights of the radiator grilles of showroom automobiles, in the elegance of the oil stains on the engine nacelles of 747s parked on airport tarmacs.

I believe in the non-existence of the past, in the death of the future, and the infinite possibilities of the present.

I believe in the derangement of the senses: in Rimbaud, William Burroughs, Huysmans, Genet, Celine, Swift, Defoe, Carroll, Coleridge, Kafka.

I believe in the designers of the Pyramids, the Empire State Building, the Berlin Fuehrerbunker, the Wake Island runways.

I believe in the body odors of Princess Di.

I believe in the next five minutes.

I believe in the history of my feet.

I believe in migraines, the boredom of afternoons, the fear of calendars, the treachery of clocks.

I believe in anxiety, psychosis and despair.

I believe in the perversions, in the infatuations with trees, princesses, prime ministers, derelict filling stations (more beautiful than the Taj Mahal), clouds and birds.

I believe in the death of the emotions and the triumph of the imagination.

I believe in Tokyo, Benidorm, La Grande Motte, Wake Island, Eniwetok, Dealey Plaza.

I believe in alcoholism, venereal disease, fever and exhaustion.

I believe in pain.

I believe in despair.

I believe in all children.

I believe in maps, diagrams, codes, chess-games, puzzles, airline timetables, airport indicator signs.

I believe all excuses.

I believe all reasons.

I believe all hallucinations.

I believe all anger.

I believe all mythologies, memories, lies, fantasies, evasions.

I believe in the mystery and melancholy of a hand, in the kindness of trees, in the wisdom of light.

.....

Originally published on March 9, 2013

06

LETTER TO JAMES GRAHAM BALLARD / APRIL 14, 2009

I wrote the following letter to James Graham Ballard on April 14, 2009, not knowing that he would die five days later, to my great sorrow.

LETTER TO JAMES GRAHAM BALLARD ///
Mumbai on Tuesday 14th April 2009

Dear Mr. Ballard,

I have some difficulty finding the right words for you; yours already reached me long time ago, allowing me to discover imaginaries that help me to comprehend better the complexit of reality. Therefore, I will use instead Emil Cioran's words in *History and Utopia* (University of Chicago Press,1998). In fact, Cioran has a way to consider the world in its ambiguity:

> Our dreams about the future cannot be unlinked anymore from what scares us. Utopic litterature's beginnings fought against Middle Age, against how this period was highly considering Hell and how it was presenting visions of the end of the world. It is likely that those systems so comforting, by Campanella or More have been conceived for the only goal of discrediting Saint Hildegarde's hallucinations. Nowadays, we are

reconciled with the notion of "terrible", we assist
to a contamination of utopia by the apocalypse:
the "new land" that has been announced is af-
fecting more and more the figuration of a new
Hell. However, we are waiting for this Hell, we
even make of a duty to accelerate its arrival. The
two types, utopic and apocalyptic which use to
appear to us as very different, are actually penetrating each other, influence one on another to
create a third one, marvelously able to reflect
the kind of reality which is threatening us et to
which we will say whatsoever, yes, a correct and
without illusion, yes. It shall be our way of being
uncorrectable in front of fatality.

You may contradict me, but I readily associate this brief and
genius brilliant passage with the spirit invigorating the totality
of your work. The ambiguity as an essence of the relationship between the human and technology exudes from this
interpretation of reality, surviving in the folds of our reality. In
this regard, what seems to be a denial of a temporality or
a territoriality within your narrative helps construct this new
imaginary. The absence of territoriality reflects an omni-ter-
ritoriality where the *homo technologicus* lives; and as far as
the absence of temporality is concerned, it seems like it allows you to blur the conceptual limits of the interpretation of
the real, the fiction and speculation. This alchemy moves us
moving towards reality as Cioran would say, experiencing it
in a perceptive jubilation.

What fascinates me in your novels, is the passionate relationship that the characters develop with technology, always
associated with the loss of control. The loss of control... It
is the core of the issue. It seems that the human jubilates in
being able to exist in an environment where his presence is

not indispensable. Does this situation alleviate his feeling of irresponsibility? Or, is it a quasi-hypnotic fascination in the face of spectacle too formidable for her/him? Or even, is it the perception that her/his existence is not necessary that allows her/him a sensation of freedom? Ambiguity derives from the fact that themselves they cannot succeed to identify the origin of such a jubilation. That may be how (s)he gradually reach to what we simplistically call "madness." To some extents, the *homo-technologicus* is constantly searching for a limit. How far can (s)he go in the loss of the control that (s)he was supposed to exercise on technology?

This loss of control actually corresponds to the condition *sine qua non* of emotion. By giving up his command, the human allows the machine to make her/him feel the vital intensity. Control was dooming the world to technocracy; its loss brings a new form of orgasm. However, there is probably no orgasm without violence; and just like any drug, its danger cannot be evacuated and its existence increases fascination. Loss of control constitutes a risk, because is contrary to certitute. In turn, certitude is contrary to the notions of surprise or event.

What would be a "psychotropic" city, if we use the same term as the one you use to describe these special houses in the short story, *The thousand dreams of Stellavista*? Transposing it to urban scale would be interesting in that it would imply a systemic logic as much as anomalies and resistances. Urban biology would only become fascinating through its behavior disturbances and its faults used by several acts of marginality that would hack a totalitarian technocratic system like the one we can see in Singapore for example.

What would be your vision of such a psychotropic city. How do you visualize this techno-ubiquity not only a system, but a fascinating field of potentials for anomalies and resistances?

My question is in the present on purpose: your vision of new imaginaries is probably inseparable from your interpretation of the reality.

Thank you very much for your time.

Léopold Lambert

.....

Originally published on November 30, 2011

07

JAMES GRAHAM BALLARD'S PSYCHOTROPIC HOUSES

The Thousand Dreams of Stellavista is a novela in the book *Vermilion Sands* written by James Graham Ballard between 1956 and 1970, and published in 1971. It centers on a peculiar type of houses that Ballard calls "psychotropic" (ethymologically: stimulated by the mind). These houses physically react to their inhabitant's mood and stress and adapt their spatiality to them.

> …it consisted of six huge aluminum-shelled spheres suspended like the elements of a mobile from an enormous concrete davit. The largest sphere contained the lounge, the others successively smaller and spiraling upward into the air, the bedrooms and kitchen…
>
> Stamers, the agent, left us sitting in the car… and switched the place on (all the houses in Vermillion Sands, it goes without saying, were psychotropic). There was a dim whirring, and the spheres tipped and began to rotate, brushing against the undergrowth.
>
> …I got out and walked over to the entrance, the main sphere slowing as I approached, uncertainly steering a course toward me, the smaller ones following.

...As I stepped forward, it jerked away, almost in alarm, the entrance retracting and sending a low shudder through the rest of the spheres.

It's always interesting to watch a psychotropic house try to adjust itself to strangers, particularly those at all guarded or suspicious. The responses vary, a blend of past reactions to negative emotions, the hostility of the previous tennants...

...Stamers was fiddling desperately with the control console recessed into the wall behind the door, damping the volume down as low as possible...

He smiled thinly at me. "Circuits are a little worn. Nothing serious..."

Similarly to most Ballardian narratives, technology is described in the context of its degeneration and loss of control. In *The Thousand Dreams of Stellavista*, the narrator buys a psychotropic house that used to belong to a couple where a wife killed her husband. The house remembers the crime and tries to reproduce its conditions in the same manner as a patient in psychoanalysis reconstitutes his/her trauma under hypnose. The narrator, prey to obsessive curiosity associated with tendency for masochism, experiences this architectural 'crisis' until its climax when the house attempts to assassinate him:

Then, abruptly, the room stilled. A second later, as I lifted myself up on one elbow, a violent spasm convulsed the room, buckling the walls and lifting the bed off the floor. The entire house

started to shake and writhe. Gripped by this sei-
zure, the bedroom contracted and expanded like
the chamber of a dying heart, the ceiling rising
and falling. (James Graham Ballard, *The Thousand Dreams of Stellavista*, in *Vermillon Sands,*
Berkley Books, 1971.)

This description of the killing house recalls the work of Eyal
Weizman about "forensic architecture" where he describes
how the Israeli and US armies engineer precise attacks that
make a part of a given building collapse to kill the target. Similarly, Bernard Tschumi in *Architecture and Disjunction* (The
MIT Press, 1996), in a chapter about architecture and sadism
wrote: "The rooms are too small or too big, the ceilings too
low or too high. Violence exercised by and through space is
spatial torture."

.....

Originally published on January 4, 2012

08

THE BRUTAL ART OF ENKI BILAL

- And that, what is it? What are we walking on?
- Canvas. White canvas… The walls and the ceiling are covered with it
- It's very nice (Enki Bilal, *32 Décembre*, Paris: Les Humanoïdes Associés, 2002.)

The *Beast Trilogy* (*The Dormant Beast, December 32nd* and *Rendez-vous in Paris*), is a series of graphic novels written and drawn by Enki Bilal, which introduces a charismatic character, Optus Warhole, who claims to be the inventor of the "Art Brutal." This terminology resonates with the notion of "Art Brut" in French ("Outsider Art" in English) invented by Jean Dubuffet in 1945. The three pieces presented in this trilogy by a character whose name is a quasi-homonym for Andy Warhol, are indeed brutal as they celebrate the creativity of destruction in a radical manner. This artistic paradox allows us to recall *On Murder Considered as one of the Fine Arts* written by Thomas de Quincey in 1827 or more recently of the remarkable character of the Joker in Christopher Nolan's *Dark Knight* in 2008.

The first of the three art pieces consists in an entire apartment covered with white canvas and in which few dozens of people completely dressed and painted in white wildly, massacre each other to provide the paint for the piece: their own blood, spurting red.

The second one materializes in the form of acid rain cloud, drifting with the wind, and whose drops pierce any matter encountered. Entitled "Compression of Eructed Death," this deadly cloud insists on the randomness of its destruction as it moves with the wind.

Finally, the third one is another cloud composed by millions of red flies which dissolve the building from which they originate. The implosion of the latter is said to have provoked a brutal sound rupture, a sort of anti-vibration that absorbs all sounds and creates multiple auditory injuries. "You are crazy" says Nike Hatzfeld to Optus Warhole in *December 32nd*. "No, I am an artist" he answers.

The following excerpts provide the description of these three art pieces directly from the graphic novels themselves (my translation):

> - For now, I mostly need to talk to a lawyer. I just committed an assassination, don't you understand?
> - Precisely, the first paintbrush strike on an immaculate canvas is always determining, that's the meaning of this murder, do you understand? Here comes the second one, look!
> - As a matter of fact, paintbrush strikes were starting to multiply everywhere. [...]

> The white canvas of the Very Great Artist named Holeraw was being rapidly covered in blood. Blood spurts, here from a slit throat, from some cut veins (there are suicides, then!), and somewhere else from some other lethal wounds. "It's beautiful, isn't it ?!" screams Pamela with a bloody knife in her hand, on her knees in front of

a young woman violently killed. "A former rival" she says.

I am curiously balanced between the desire to throw up and burst into laughter. [...]

Holographic unfolding of the three rooms *All White Happening* by Optus Warhole (Holeraw). 87 participants, 61 deaths. One can notice that the victims' blood marks compose the artist's signature.

(Click on the blood stains to see the murders) [...]

First, there was a loud roar, not the thunder, nothing really identifiable. Then, a pestilential smell spread out in the cold air, exhaled from the sepulchral mouth.

Black drops fell on faces. [...]

- Given the scream you just uttered, you must have seen the thing and smelled. It is a shame that my own perception has been that mediocre. I must be able to improve the system

- What was this horror?

- *Compression of Eructed Death*. My very last piece. You don't like it? It will propagate in the form of a compact cloud following the winds or my own will. Before disagregating, it will weep rain from the decomposition of two million soldiers and civilians dead on the field of bullshit...

It's an universal piece against war and men's blindness. Nevertheless, it will be destructive. The boomerang effect, I suppose.

This is not Art Brut [Outsider Art], this is Art Brutal. [...]

Dozens of bodies were shaking in pain. The critiques' delegation seemed to be the most affected. The black rain drops were piercing everything they were touching, and I strongly believe that some people died. [...]

Death Cloud
Active cloud above Kuala Lumpur
International institutions' scientists and military, in charge to contain the *Compression of Eructed Death*, phenomenon/art piece claimed by Optus Warhole, have difficulties to find a collective strategy. The last time it was seen, the death cloud was more than two kilometers long and the pestilential rains' rate was increasing. Let's remind everybody that standard umbrellas are in no way useful. There are hundreds of victims. It recently rained on a Japanese neo-nuclear plant.

Gangrenous Art
Joao Mendez-Coe, Independent Art Critic, assisted Optus Warhole's murderous happening (*Compression of Erupted Death*); twelve casualties among the spectators and seven among art critics. Her face was injured, her right collarbone and both her hands. She gives us a pertinent and evolutive analysis of Warhole's work that, she claims, is part of now as a gangrenous element according to her own terminology. (Enki Bilal, *32 Décembre*, Paris: Les Humanoïdes Associés, 2002.)

Optus Warhole. Art Work Suicide
Holeraw posing in front of the dissolution of his

own building during the Brutal Silence Phenomenon. *Red (Red Der Decompression)* penetrates into the *Black (Compression of Eructed Death)*.

Red Der Decompression in Bangkok
This happening has been followed by several thousand people on site, by hundreds of millions of other on television, and by a selection of ninety nine international art critics from the top of the Oriental Peninsula hotel with the artist himself. (Enki Bilal, *Rendez-vous à Paris*, Paris: Les Humanoïdes Associés, 2002.)

.....

Originally published on July 16, 2011

09

THE WORK OF PHILIP K. DICK: BETWEEN PARANOIA AND SCHIZOPHRENIA

If one were compelled to categorize science fiction works, we could distinguish between the machinist fascination of Jules Verne and H.G. Wells, the epic interstellar narratives and the speculative robotic would be led by Isaac Asimov, the descriptions of the alien as the essential undescriptable by Stanislaw Lem, and finally the co-existence of overlapping worlds and the entropy to which these worlds are subjected by Philip K. Dick. Dick's novels and novelas focus on the absolute uncertainty of the main characters concerning their identity as well as the tangibility of the world that surrounds them.

Much as I love Ridley Scott's *Blade Runner* as an adaptation of Dick's *Do Androids Dream of Electric Sheep* (1968), it misses one of the fundamental points of the book: the absolute horror that one experiences when (s)he realize that all her/his memory have been programmed in her/his brain and that instead of being a human, (s)he is actually an android. Similarly, the ambiguity that surrounds the main character, Rick Deckard and his potential androidness is not as poignant in the film as it is in the novel:

> "An android," he said, "doesn't care what happens to any other android. That's one of the indi-

cations we look for."

"Then," Miss Luft said, "you must be an android."

That stopped him; he stared at her.

"Because," she continued, "Your job is to kill them, isn't it? You're what they call — " She tried to remember.

"A bounty hunter," Rick said. "But I'm not an android."

"This test you want to give me." Her voice, now, had begun to return. "Have you taken it?"

"Yes." He nodded. "A long, long time ago; when I first started with the department."

"Maybe that's a false memory. Don't androids sometimes go around with false memories?"
(Philip K. Dick, *Do Androids Dream of Electric Sheep*, Del Rey, 1996.)

In *Time out of Joint* (1959), *The Man in the High Castle* (1962), *Martian Time-slip* (1964), *Ubik* (1969), *Flow My Tears, the Policeman Said* (1974) Philip K. Dick describes worlds superimposed on the vision of the main characters in order to deceive them about what the reality truly is — although this reality might also be an illusive layer. For example, *The Man in the High Castle* introduces the United States as they have been shared by Japan and the Third Reich after they won the second world war. In the story, a book *The Grasshopper Lies Heavy* describes a world in which the Allies won the war. For the readers of Dick's books, the fact that the protagonists eventually realizes that their reality is hiding ours reinforces the doubt that our reality might very well be hiding theirs.

Nevertheless, Philip K. Dick does not limit his deceiving realities hypotheses to his fictions. On the contrary, he never missed an occasion to emit doubts about the reality of our world in the various interviews he gives, as well as in his well-known lecture at the Metz Science Fiction Festival in 1977, *If You Find this World Bad You Should See Some of the Others*. In this text, he implies that the current world where we live is a counterfeit reality to hide the fact that we are still living during the 1st century and that we are all persecuted Christians by the Roman Empire, embodied in this reality by Richard Nixon and his administration. As always, wondering about whether or not Dick was serious is irrelevant: only the doubt that he manages to create matters.

In 1978, Philip K. Dick writes a text humorously entitled *How to Build a Universe that Doesn't Fall Apart Two Days Later* in which he evokes his predilection for the creation of parallel realities. This title is misleading, however, since what he is precisely interested in is the description of the erosion or entropy of these realities. The character of the schizophrenic in his novels is the entity able to see beyond the appearance, in the dusty and muddy eroded entrails of the reality:

> Contemplating Dr. Glaub sitting opposite him, Jack Bohlen felt the gradual diffusion of his perception which he so dreaded, the change in his awareness which had attacked him this way years ago in the personnel manager's office at Corona Corporation, and which always seemed still with him, just on the edge.
> He saw the psychiatrist under the aspect of absolute reality: a thing composed of cold wires and switches, not a human at all, not made of flesh. The fleshy trappings melted and became transparent, and Jack Bohlen saw the mechanical device beyond. (Philip K. Dick, *Martian Time Slip*, Del Rey, 1992.)

In *Ubik*, Dick dramatizes two contradictory forces fighting against each other. While the reality seems to be subjected to a chronological entropy that makes each object and body regress in time from a futuristic 1992 to the beginning of the 1950s, the product *Ubik*, on the contrary, tends to reverse time to its 'normal' course.

The paroxysm of this entropy can be read in *Do Androids Dream of Electric Sheep*, which enunciates the Law of Kipple, a neologism invented by Dick to describe the force that subjects all objects and bodies to an eventual return to the state of dust. In this regard, the biblical "All came from dust and will return to dust" would probably not be refused by him.

> "Kipple is useless objects, like junk mail or match folders after you use the last match or gum wrappers or yesterday's homeopape. When nobody's around, kipple reproduces itself. For instance, if you go to bed leaving any kipple around your apartment, when you wake up the next morning there's twice as much of it. It always gets more and more."
>
> "I see." The girl regarded him uncertainly, not knowing whether to believe him. Not sure if he meant it seriously.
>
> "There's the First Law of Kipple," he said. "'Kipple drives out nonkipple.' Like Gresham's law about bad money. And in these apartments there's been nobody there to fight the kipple."
>
> "So it has taken over completely," the girl finished. She nodded. "Now I understand."
>
> "Your place, here," he said, "this apartment you've picked — it's too kipple-ized to live in. We can roll the kipple-factor back; we can do like I said, raid the other apts. But — " He broke off.
>
> "But what?"

Isidore said, "We can't win."

"Why not? The girl stepped into the hall, closing the door behind her; arms folded selfconsciously before her small high breasts she faced him, eager to understand. Or so it appeared to him, anyhow. She was at least listening.

"No one can win against kipple," he said, "except temporarily and maybe in one spot, like in my apartment I've sort of created a stasis between the pressure of kipple and nonkipple, for the time being. But eventually I'll die or go away, and then the kipple will again take over.

It's a universal principle operating throughout the universe; the entire universe is moving toward a final state of total, absolute kippleization." (Philip K. Dick, *Do Androids Dream of Electric Sheep*, Del Rey, 1996.)

.....

Originally published on March 4, 2012

10

THE FUNAMBULIST PAPERS 03: TRANSCENDENT DELUSION OR; THE DANGEROUS FREE SPACES OF PHILIP K. DICK BY MARTIN BYRNE

[also in The Funambulist Papers: Volume 1 (Punctum, 2013)]

Following the previous chapter's evocation of the concepts of kipple and gubble invented by Philip K. Dick, I am adding another perspetive than mine here:

TRANSCENDENT DELUSION OR; THE DANGEROUS FREE SPACES OF PHILIP K. DICK ///
By Martin Byrne

(Solo queda / el desierto.)[1]

You find yourself walking through a long dusty corridor in a dank building sometime in the late afternoon. The doors to nearly every room have long since fallen in, letting pale shafts of light mingle with dust and paper; assorted debris whirls about in lazy semi-circles as you pass quietly by. There are no lights apart from the fading sun; there is no sound except for the slow pacing of your own feet and the idle mixed thoughts that bounce from left to right in your head. The fur-

1 Fredercio Garcia Lorca, *And Then, from Poem of the Deep Song,* San Francisco: City Lights Publishers, 2001.

ther you walk down the corridor, the more overwhelming your sense of isolation becomes. Through each doorway you see rooms that have been long forgotten; weeds sprouting from moldy ephemera in the foreground and a long view out of the broken floor-to-ceiling windows beyond. Each frame you pass in steady syncopation offers a glimpse of what seems to be an encroaching desert. Shifting piles of dust cover in fits and starts the remains of a world that you never found entirely familiar to begin with.

How do you feel?

If you at all feel anxious, dirty, or alone, it might be wise for you to stop reading now. "And why are you anxious about clothing? Consider well the lilies of the field, how they grow.[2]" Or, I should say, in the Phillip K. Dick universe: 'And why are you anxious about architecture? Consider the kipple of the world, how it spreads.' For therein lies your salvation. Also, before I continue, if you have not read Martian Time-Slip nor Do Androids Dream of Electric Sheep? I suggest you stop whatever you're doing and go read these novels. Simultaneously, multiple times in a row.

Now, over the course of the varied and illuminated career of science fiction writer Phillip K Dick, we follow the author and his hapless characters through a veritable labyrinth of shifting worlds, be they physical or mental, most in some stage of degradation and decrepitude, perhaps in some way similar to the scene described above. Often within these worlds, Dick wields his God-given-right-to-naming through the creation of a few choice words that might describe these decaying worlds and all their subtle majesty. The two neologisms that seem to have the most potential are kipple and gubble, which vaguely signify physical shifts and mental shifts, re-

2 Matthew 6:28

spectively. It is my contention that the author uses these two terms with a secondary, perhaps unintentional, function within his narratives. Dick's complimentary concepts of kipple and gubble are both the devices and scenarios with which and in which his characters find solace and transcendence from their increasingly apathetic environments. The characters exist within fundamentally unbalanced societies that they manage to escape by occupying the spaces and mentalities of kipple and gubble.

First, both kipple and gubble are functions that involve members of society who are cast-off, forgotten, or are otherwise undesirable. Kipple occupies the physical domain of the chickenheads, antheads, other pea-brained humans, and, of course, the fleeing androids in Do Androids and it is perpetually encroaching. Gubble is the mental space of the autistic and the physical space of the Bleekman (Martians) in Martian Time-Slip. What is interesting to note is that these people and environments have been deemed inherently incompatible with the rest of society, and yet it is here that they either induce or are indicative of moments of transcendence for the protagonists. Take for example the case of JR Isidore, the golden-hearted chickenhead who first introduces us to kipple in Do Androids. Living nearly in "the wastes," JR finds himself almost entirely alone in an abandoned conapt [a neologism of lesser strength] where kipple encroaches from all sides. This is also the place where he happens, astoundingly, to find a live spider, eking out a living on Dick-knows-what. Combine this awe-inspiring and unfathomably rare occurrence with Rick Deckard's discovery of a 'Toad (Bufonidae), all varieties…….E.' (E for extinct) in the desert as he is contemplating suicide, and you have twice witnessed the strongest of many other subtle experiences these characters are allowed to have precisely in a space that is dismissed by their society proper as being a wasteland. These kinds of characters are written off as delusional, the spaces they inhabit are alien and hostile, and yet they happen across transcendence that other characters crave but never find. (It is also interesting to note that the characters that Dick highlights as insatiate are often the wives of the protagonists. In Do Androids Deckard's wife often considers suicide and has a troubled relationship with her mood organ while in Martian, Bohlen's wife is addicted to Phenobarbitals and views her world through a perpetually glassy-eyed haze.)

Now, when dealing with transcendence, one cannot forget the figure of Wilbur Mercer (who was egregiously omitted from the film adaptation.) Wilbur Mercer is the figure-head of the spiritual movement in Do Androids, and is accessed through an 'empathy box.' What we find intriguing about this motif is that the mood organ transports the users via hologram of some sort into what the society inherently fears: the desert, the wasteland, the place where kipple has taken over entirely. It is within this space, the desert, the kipple-space, that they seek to be one with each other. It is here that they deactivate their robotic, mood-organ-dictated "feelings" and open themselves to true empathy and their own deep humanity once more. The irony that robots are being hunted for being 'too human' is as palpable as ersatz sheep's wool, which is to say 'exceedingly so'.

Beyond this, we enter the world of gubbish. Here we can begin to see the confluence of architecture and mental deviance, and how Dick often aligns the two. What is interesting in this analysis is that the persons involved with the architectural and mental deviations are children, but that is for another time perhaps. In Martian Time-Slip, there are two children who occupy the two poles of a diagnostic society; one is the protagonist's son, David, and the other is the neighbors' son, Manfred. David is perfectly adjusted to being brought up on Mars, according to the colony's conceptions of being well-adjusted. (His own mother claims that he was "trained to say no," and that he was at the top of his school class. Not a positive distinction. We later learn that the schooling system trains the children to be followers, repeating canned answers with no chance for variation or digression. Remind you of anything?) Manfred, however, is autistic and cannot become a 'functioning member of society.' Additionally, each boy is represented by a certain architecture; David, the public school, and Manfred, the desert. The public school, as described in the thoughts of the protagonist:

> "It was a battle, Jack realized between the composite psyche of the school and the individual psyches of the children, and the former held all the key cards. A child who did not properly respond was assumed to be autistic – that is, oriented according to a subjective factor that took precedence over his sense of objective reality. And that child wound up by being expelled from the school; he went, after that, to another school entirely, one designed to rehabilitate him: he went to Camp Ben-Gurion. He could not be taught; he could only be dealt with as ill.[3]"

We learn that these two children are also indicative of the two types of people who populate the Martian colonies. You are either a complete neurotic, which is accepted as normal and subsequently heavily medicated with all manner of phenobarbitals and Dexamye [recall Bohlen's wife]. Or you are of a 'schizoid temperament,' and shipped off to a 'camp' in New Israel to be 'dealt with.' At the climax of the book, these two conditions are brought together when the protagonist begins to experience his previously suppressed schizophrenic

3 Dick, Phillip K. Martian Time-Slip, New York: Random House Digital, Inc., 1995.

episodes in concert with Manfred within the public school, within the architecture of the opposite mentality. These two mentalities collide and cause Bohlen's world to devolve into gubbish talk and gubbled environments, where bones burst through skin and buildings reach out to cut you, while Manfred's world blossoms in the slow graceful movement of the Bleekman, with whom he can now miraculously converse telepathically. Previously, Manfred was only vaguely aware of the humans he was surrounded by daily, in an environment that he consistently described as sharp and hostile, in his quiet narration. And throughout all of this, Manfred intermittently experiences time-slips where he is forced to witness a potential future of his; he is trapped in a decaying retirement home while attached to an unholy array of machinery that keeps him alive in a state of deranged torture.

In Dick's masterful resolution, we find the characters confronting all of these mental deviations on sacred Bleekman ground in a shallow cave in the bleak Martian desert, affectionately known as Dirty Knobby. Again, it is here in the inhospitable, entirely alien, and patently dangerous desert that Manfred's consciousness comes into conflict with the symbol of extreme neuroses one Arnie Kott, and achieves a sort of transcendence after which Manfred is able to communicate and eventually live with the Bleekman permanently. His terrifying visions of the future decaying building transform into a pleasant life of wandering in the desert (and smoking cigarettes) with the Bleekman. It seems as though his immersion the gubbish world was only achievable through his schizoid temperament through which he was able to escape a neurotic society to find solace in the desert.

> "Perhaps, for the first time in his life, the boy was in a situation to which he might make an adjustment; he might, with the wild Bleekman, discern

a style of living which was genuinely his and not a pallid, tormented reflection of the lives of those around him, beings who were innately different from him and whom he could never resemble, no matter how hard he tried.[4]"

We should all be so lucky. Folie à plusieurs, I suppose? Now how do you feel?

.....

Originally published on July 11, 2011

---

4 Ibid.

11

UNTITLED NARRATIVE #002 (FERAL GARAGE) BY MARTIN BYRNE

It seems appropriate for a book about science fiction to include at least one fictitious piece to complement more analytical writings. The following narrative is written by Martin Byrne (see also the previous chapter), he describes a character experencing a building that develops a feral condition through a dysfunction of its technological system.

This narrative takes place in an architecture also conceived by Byrne. His inspiration starts from the observation of IBM recent advertising for a so-called "smarter planet," hosting the ubiquity of sensors and interactive devices. One understands how a corporation like IBM could be economically interested in proposing such a vision of the world in association with governmental institutions that would see in this program an opportunity to increase their control over populations. Byrne's architecture is a parking garage "dialoguing" with its non-identical twin server tower in Mid-Town Manhattan. Both towers have been fictitiously designed for IBM: the server one remains a pristine universe; however, the over-magnetic charge of the sensors in the parking garage building makes it "go back" to a feral state, where unexpected forms of life start to develop. Humans are then invited to negotiate with their own fear to enter this building that developed its own form of uncontrol.

UNTITLED NARRATIVE # 002 ///
by Martin Byrne (including previous image)

001

April is the cruelest month.

Sitting rigidly at the far end of the thick clear plastic conference table – enameled and embossed with desaturated flickering figures, charts, and graphs – nervous little Eli Warring
was sweating under the weight of the expectations recently
laid upon him. Only six weeks a freshman at the firm, he had
yet to witness such a large and encompassing responsibility
delegated to someone as unsullied as himself, regardless of
the sufficiency of the intellect within. Wiping the moisture from
his palms onto his Bergdorf-patterned knees, he tried not to
look at the flexing, intelligent walls streaming with data like
rivulets of pixilated water – wary that they may register some
sense of the fear he was attempting so desperately to hide.
The neuroses from which he had suffered since his hermetic
childhood came rushing forward into his face, filling his eyes,
ears, and nose with blood in sharp triangles of anxiety and
heat. He thought vaguely of the cold white playroom of his
youth that had been kept ordered and clean – a premedi-
tated training ground for productive development. While the
right side of his brain idly recalled the quiet clean uneventful
space, the left rationally processed the instructions, require-
ments, and directions he was being spoon-fed by the various
consultants. The blood slowly receded and he prayed that
the disembodied heads on suspended plastic conferencing
screens hadn't noticed his mental deviance from the task at
hand.

"Now, if you follow these numbers, it seems everything was
going as expected," exasperated, Sofie Powers exhaled

roughly. She flicked her empty left hand out towards Eli – fingers gracefully poised like those of a dismissive dancer – sending a small chart skittering through the electronic ether of the table. It came to rest perfectly square in front of him, overlaying the other information he was supposed to be retaining. Sofie Powers was not pleased with the situation at hand and made it more than evident. With her thumb and forefinger she rubbed her forehead, eventually looking up towards Eli with an elongated sigh. He forced a serious grimace and nodded.

"We have the collective monitoring data from each separate system relayed to the central processing core. All of the systems report fluctuation within the expected parameters, yet somehow the whole thing still turned into this nightmare," she continued, dropping her hand-held tablet brusquely onto the desk in a digital splash of connecting reference points and tabulated flow charts. The frameless plastic hit the table with a hollow sound and sent percentages, probabilities and complex algorithms flitting from screen to screen, alighting across the stern and severe visages of those physically present. The video-conferenced heads in turn became slightly obscured by the intrusion of graphs on their screens – ersatz veils coloring already detached minds. Strong blue and green hues reflected off of sharp cheekbones and well-exercised jaw lines. Eli worried his face reflected the putrid yellow-grey bile that was increasingly gathering in his quivering abdomen.

Turning to one of the suspended screens, Sofie asked pointedly, "Bill, when you were last in the labs, did it at all show signs of failure?" She leaned slightly to the left and tapped her finger upon her slight cheekbone, lost in some internal thought process, clearly not listening to the forthcoming response.

"No, ma'am. Not in the slightest. I was surveying the progress in Lab 607.A and it seemed under control and regimented as always. Their hourly reports also reflected zero inconsistencies. Everything was perfect." Bill continued to rattle off the statistics of Lab 607.A's perfection at length. Eli focused with difficulty and found himself surprisingly eager to wander through the condemned depths of this recently toxic site. It had been a mere month since the new research headquarters had opened at 59th and 5th to an almost ludicrously loud largesse, and it had met this wondrous opening with an equally grand and magnificent collapse. The fanfare had been showered on the triumph of a million brilliant minds that had come together in the harmony of scientific perfection; its future seemed as promising as the advertising campaigns had promised. This single edifice was to be the shining, shimmering beacon of the instrumented, interconnected, and intelligent world to come. It had been meticulously worked and re-worked, poured over for years by the scientists, analysts, engineers and information architects of the IBM Corporation. Humankind was on the verge of witnessing the bright and glittering daybreak of a terrifyingly intelligent planet. Little did IBM know, its masterpiece was about to fall headlong into the shadow that daybreak inevitably brings.

(Come in under the shadow of this red rock.)

The masterpiece consisted of forty stories of intelligent opaque glass – a crystalline research and development facility so advanced the entirety of its interior was held to the unprecedented clean room laboratory standards. In order to achieve the ideal interior lab environment, each floor had been outfitted with an entry decontamination chamber that served as the transition between the public parking deck and the lab spaces themselves. The building's immense mechanical service core was isolated from the laboratories within the parking deck to ensure the perfect and unadulterated operation of the rest of the facility. The heart serving – but not influencing – the brain. But the true soul of the building came from its instrumentation – the devices that would count the sheep of the dormant machine. In a glorious symphony of input and output relays generated by an unfathomable amount of sensors, the building was able to read every minute action of each system and occupant to a degree never previously possible. A faint blue wave swept over instruments, faucets, tensed shoulder blades, and nimble fingers reading and calculating radiated heat, wasted chemicals, and completed tasks. The entirety of this information was registered, parsed, and analyzed in a database so immense it could only be contained in a massive server farm far below the surface – data as the frigid foundation of the future. IBM had intended this facility to be the symbolic head in the quest for complete knowledge in every possible sense, and its digestion of the world into mere data was the lynchpin of it all. No stone left unturned. No shadow left unlit.

Looking into the heart of light, the silence,

And yet, the utter desolation it had wrought upon itself had been so complete and complex, the EPA had no choice but to immediately render the entire block a Superfund site and delay its demolition until the responsible party had undertaken a full retrospective evaluation. From the brief reports that were successfully uploaded prior to and during failure, advanced analysts were able to witness the internal intelligence of the design operating its absolute highest capacity. It was here, at the height of its success and at the absolute optimum levels of operation, that its inevitable failure made itself known. While the IBM Advanced Research Facility was functioning at its highest possible capacity, it was also unwittingly creating its most perfect disaster. Those exact functions that kept the clean rooms clean, the data feeds efficient, the water pure, were simultaneously creating a serious of environments that should have never come into being. The loop was closed, the system was as internalized as it could possibly have been. And yet it seemed, from preliminary reports, that those systems there were employed to keep the place alive were exactly the systems that caused its untimely death. How this was at all possible, was still in question. Enter, stage right, the International Business Machine Corporation and its lowly and voluntary servant, one Eli Warring – who sat chewing his soft nails and bouncing his knobby knees in apprehension of documenting the disaster that lay before him in its manifestly glorious ruin.

Breeding lilacs out of dead land,

"Alright, thank you, Bill. Your point has been made. Now, Eli, are you clear on the full extent of your responsibilities? I believe the preliminary staging report was given to you yesterday. Is that correct?" Ms. Powers interjected, startling both Bill and Eli alike.

"Yes, yes ma'am. After I received it, I promptly re-ordered my action item list to correspond with the minutes the report described." Eli shifted slightly in his chair, automatically running through the list he had memorized out of fear.

"Good. Now, it's a simple task, albeit lengthy, that only requires you follow the directions given. Is that clear?"

Son of man, You cannot say, or guess,

for you only know, a heap of broken images,

"Yes ma'am."

"Unfortunately, the EPA has limited our access to the site, so you'll have to do this all in one shot, start to finish. You'll be allowed entrance at six o'clock tomorrow morning."

"Yes ma'am."
"Alright, thank you everybody. We'll meet again in two days when Eli returns."

I was neither living nor dead, and I knew nothing,

002

With a wicked pack of cards. Here, said she,

Is your card, the drowned Phoenician Sailor,

The southern portion of the massive edifice seemed too heavy for the ground, sinking slightly here and there, crushing itself under its own gargantuan mass. Concrete splinters projected out at angles, some appearing to be downspouts from which streams of water intermittently poured. Over-hanging ledges were saturated in thick heavy vines, dangling in putrid clumps. Large fissures gaped from mangled corners, awaiting the arrival of some nesting bird or a drifting piece of debris to lodge itself amongst the crumbling concrete and exposed rebar. Small strange metal trusses grew out of the concrete like the spines of a manic cactus, mostly crusted over at their sharp tips, all leaden in a vile-looking green covering. Several large, vaguely rectangular masses of concrete pulled themselves considerable distances from the southern and eastern facades, not one less than four stories tall. Rusted I-beams pierced the lumpy surface at random, disturbing the brown streams of water that trickled down to splash wildly onto the sidewalk below. The whole place resembled some kind of deranged hanging garden. An overwhelming sense of dread began form like a distant thundercloud in the dark corners of Eli's mind.

At the weed matted overhang that marked the entrance to the parking garage, Eli disappeared slowly into shadow with a prolonged and shaky exhale. Out of the corner of his eye, he noticed a thin grey wisp of smoke drift lazily past his taught face. He held his breath and inched forwards one slow step at a time. He gulped down a quick breath that made him cringe and he spat heavily onto the ground to rid the sweet unfamiliar taste of rot and unfiltered air from his lungs. His eyes slowly adjusted to the dim blue light emanating from damaged sensors that hung immense in their overgrown frames. The pale blue sensor light mixed unevenly with the hazy moss-colored fumes that wafted about his shoulders, unevenly streaming from large grates in the ground that lay between him and the main entrance of the laboratory. A strange and unexpected sense of longing crept over him to feel the heat and warmth the exhaust might offer.

Under the brown fog of a winter dawn,

He shook this thought from his head as quickly as it had entered. The backpack he had been given when leaving the office that morning felt heavy about his shoulders; he slipped his thumbs under the straps and readjusted it onto his already perspiring back. Walking forward into the dim misty light, he passed through a series of sensor gates meant to register the entry, speed, make, model, and condition of every car that traversed under their unwavering gaze. Eli felt a strange pang of excitement, as if he was exploring the tomb of some long lost civilization, secrets and mysteries behind every corner, under every rock, between every crevice. For the first time since he had been assigned his duties, he smiled.

By the time he had reached the center of the immensely tall central atrium, his head had tilted all the way back to stare at the dense equipment that was arranged almost haphazardly in the air above his head. "Wow," he said out loud to the creeping plants and misty ether. Though he had known better, the concrete seemed solid from the exterior – from here, it proved only to be a rather thin shell. The ramping square spiral parking deck wound its way up and around a central core of colossal machines, some whirring, others hanging idly from substantial steel cables. Variously sized pipes and fat wires criss-crossed between machines, down through chases in the concrete and upwards into vapor. Through the haze Eli could also make out a winding catwalk that disappeared behind a mysteriously blank metal surface only to emerge again at the level of the concourse above, where a gate sagged on broken metal hinges. A perverse to dash off to explore this bizarre cadre of environments overwhelmed him so strongly that he could not resist darting off through the pathetic undergrowth towards the wide-open ramp of the first concourse.

As he trotted up the sloping metal grating that formed the parking deck, he became aware of the weight and sound of his own footsteps for the first time – sharp clangs rang out with every step he took. Never had he sensed the significance of his own presence in a place, nor had the potential of his own body felt so immediate and overwhelming.

"Speak to me. Why do you never speak? Speak.

A voice pierced his senses, coming in short bursts from the wireless earbud he had planted in his ear before setting off.

"Eli, its Paige. We just received an update from the EPA. They're going to spray down the site with that containment spray they've been using. Ms. Powers says that you'll have to cut out Sections D, K, and P, and to double-time it on the rest. You've got to be out by midnight Wednesday instead of 6am Thursday. Got it?"

"Yes, I understand. Does she know how difficult that – "
"We'll keep you updated. Thanks."

With a slight click Eli found himself alone again. More or less. He was leaning on a warm concrete column that rose lazily into the steam above his head. Eli had only gone up a single ramp, most likely no higher than fifteen feet off the ground. Directly in front of his vacant gaze was the still shimmering glass façade of the laboratory tower.

"What is that noise?"

Without warning, the salty tinge of human sweat and metallic blood crept into his senses; his childish urge to go exploring vanished instantly. He imagined the decaying corpse of some poor soul that had become trapped within the vines – a maintenance man, perhaps, that had succumbed to the sly and deadly will formed from the life of the weeds and the strength of the machines. The storm cloud of dread grew in his mind as the environment slowly turned on him. No longer did it promise the joy of discovery, rather it held in vicious shadows unknown threats and treacherously sharp edges. The clouds of steam seemed to follow and lick about the corners of his mouth attempting to infiltrate his lungs as he moved through the undergrowth of errant weeds and lurid vines that seemed to beset him from all sides. Diseased spores grew in great uneven, ragged clumps around the sharp angular concrete walls of the parking deck, threatening to get loose and become lodged within his throat. Eli looked frantically about and felt the ramps being choked by a torrent of plant-life that was nearly luminescent in its rancidness. The building was being devoured from within by a flurry of tumor-like growths and foul mechanic byproducts. And here he stood, alone in the middle of it all.

I think we are in rats' alley
Where the dead men lost their bones.

003

HURRY UP PLEASE ITS TIME

Fearing the supernatural combination of weed and machine would consume him; Eli had dashed off without a thought as to where he was going. He now found himself several concourses further up the ramp and entirely embedded within the threatening structure. He had felt the overwhelming claustrophobia brought on by the fear-induced illusion that everything was reaching out from him – grasping at his throat, clawing at his face, breathing on his neck. Serotonin and adrenaline soaked into the folds of his brain from his brief run and with the aid of these chemicals, he eventually calmed down. With a few rapid blinks, his curiosity and will to explore bloomed again.

'This place is crazy. What is wrong with me?' he thought. He shook his head a few times and swung his backpack around to take out his remote sensing equipment. Perhaps that would provide an answer. He fumbled with the switches until a beep let him know that it was running. Pellets of color showed on the screen, much the way a childhood toy of his had done, each dot tracing the wire frame of everything around him. A complete three-dimensional scan of the building was being compiled in pixels, one at a time. As he stared intensely at the small screen, he could make out nothing that he couldn't see with his naked eye. Perhaps a mechanism within the grey water tanks that he didn't recognize, but not much else. No sign of anyone. No rotting corpse, nothing to fear. Stumped, Eli pushed a series of buttons until he thought the device had been turned off. With a slight heave, he slung the backpack on and decided that he should get to work on the water tank logs. He would have to venture out onto a derelict catwalk but perhaps from there he could get a better vantage point.

Pressing lidless eyes and waiting for a knock upon the door.

Walking over to the small gate, Eli looked out towards the grey water tanks that floated almost weightlessly in the thick humid air. Intrigued by their foamy contents, he pushed the gate aside and took a few short steps onto the metal grille. Just as he did so, the grating dropped ever so slightly. His hands shot out to the railings and he bent his knees bracing for an impact that never came. Opening only one eye, he saw that the catwalk had only shifted under his small frame. 'I must be crazy,' he thought to himself. 'This is not me. I would never do something like this. This damn thing is going to fall and I'm going to die. What is this place doing to me? Am I talking to myself now, too?' Eli found he had become of two minds since he had started out. One sent him sprawling out like a child thrown into an unknown, utterly mysterious, and completely dangerous environment, while the other tried to protect him from that environment by over-loading his brain with fear. 'This is ridiculous,' he thought. 'Just go grab the water table logs and get off this damn thing.'
While I was fishing in the dull canal

Eli took two more small steps and immediately heard a loud cracking sound. Whipping his head left and right, he saw a vine that had wrapped itself around the railing of the catwalk breaking in sinewy threads. Some unknown instinct spun him on his heel and sent him leaping back towards the gate not five feet away. The force of his push tore through the few remaining threads of vine and sent a section of the catwalk crashing down through the closest water tank in a spray of vile yellow shards of glass. It plummeted further down, catching the cables of an air handler, tearing them loose from their mountings. The air handler swung violently across the void and crashed into the parking deck, rending a hole in the metal decking and blocking the rest of the way down. Eli had managed to catch the lower rung of access ladder, and had hung there watching. With a huge groan and wild thrashing of his legs, he managed to roll back onto the decking where he had started. He could do nothing but lay there, breathing in short bursts and staring wild-eyed at the ceiling of the next deck. A huge wave of exhaustion over took him while he lay on the deck, enticing him to close his eyes for a moment. The adrenaline that had propelled him off the catwalk fled from his fingertips and left him feeling nothing but empty. He blinked slowly, and felt the world darken around him.

The nymphs are departed.

Eli's body twitched in tension as he awoke. Startled that he had dozed off, his nerves began to relay more information than they had ever known. He was being chewed raw by this inhospitable place, and his consciousness came to him in waves. It was no longer the anxiety he had felt in what seemed like a distant past, but rather an acute awareness of the present. Like a deer standing in a smoldering sylvan glen, he moved to crouch amongst concrete pillars, ready at a moments notice to fly into action. Sharpened, he discovered instincts he had not known existed; perhaps the days spent in board meetings haggling over the most pedantic of legal contracts had hinted at a persistence of will that now seemed almost preternatural. And when it mattered most, it had bloomed in full.

One of the low on whom assurance sits

Small ragged slivers of sunlight cut through the damp darkness around where he crouched, suggesting that a significant amount of time had passed since he had entered. If the sun was this low in the sky, he would not have much time to finish his work and find a way out before his deadline came. Nonetheless, Eli felt satisfied to simply sit in this broken environment and take it in. Closing his eyes, Eli sighed and listened to water dripping in slow echoing bursts from the lumpy concrete walls; it washed in streams down columns into low basins where it found its way down the interior stairwells. Moss grew in lazy soft clumps on the northern edges of inverted speed bumps; effectively depressions in the ground where massive puddles were collecting – antediluvian beasts swimming therein, he was certain. It struck him as odd that as he ascended higher and higher into the parking deck he still felt deep within a cavern. Glancing upwards to gauge how much farther the roof was, he noticed that as it rose higher the concrete that encased the stairwells and columns eventually seemed to carve itself off the steel structure beneath. It was as if gravity were pulling the concrete downwards to leave rusting steel beams and columns to rise up like a corpse shedding its threadbare skin.

And walked among the lowest of the dead

"Eli! Its Paige, what's going on? Where are your reports? Ms. Powers is losing it over here. We've been trying to contact you for hours!" Eli jumped in surprise and whipped his head about looking for his assailant, only to remember the earbud in his left ear.

"I – what? Oh, well I've hit a few snags here and there. This place is stranger than we thought." He stuttered and tried to fabricate some excuse.

"I don't care how strange it is, Ms. Powers is flipping out on me because of you! So, get yourself together and start responding to us and submitting your reports!" A hard burst of static pummeled his ear and let him know that Paige had slammed down her receiver. He was left standing exasperated and confused.

In a feeble attempt to keep up with the charge he had been given a lifetime ago, Eli swung his torn backpack from his shoulder and rummaged around for the small remote sensing equipment he had yet to fully figure out. Pressing the small red power switch, he aimed what he thought was the sensor head towards the concrete stairwells, slowly panning into the central void of the parking structure. The equipment let off satisfied beeps and blips, as it traced the outlines of the massive machinery that kept the adjacent laboratory functioning at its highest capacity. Still whirring, air condensers flitted across the minute screen in pintilized abstractions, replete with the lumps of moss and vines that had grown around the humidity and moisture from the waste heat recovery vents. The water tanks that hung heavily from their steel mountings on concrete platforms above swirled with their foul contents, algae registering in vile yellow masses on his equipment. Above and to Eli's left, hung rotten HEPA filters like a barbarian display of defeated enemies' corpses, lined in rows showing their various states of degradation. Eli could only guess that they had been hung in such a manner to dried by the hot air and scraped clean at a later date. Evidently the maintenance crew had not reached that stage by the time they were forced to leave.

He recorded for a few minutes more, trying to capture the complex absurdity of the place, but the smell began to make his eyes water. Clicking the remote sensing equipment off, he clumsily stuffed it back into his bag. Looking over the edge, he stared down the long staggered hole in the decking full of machinery until it began to affect his sense of balance. Nervous little Eli Warring pulled himself upright using the inner rail of the concourse, wiped at his mouth, and decided to move on.

To Carthage then I came

Getting to the top of the ninth concourse, Eli stopped. A large blue van lay on its side, a mangled heap of shattered glass and creepers blocking the path upwards. Small pieces of circuitry were scattered across the decking, and Eli could only guess that it had been some type of electronics delivery gone horribly awry. Stepping closer to the wreckage, he noticed dark chunks of rubber from the tires in the decking. The van had been going up the ramp. He thought to himself that it must have been going at an incredible speed and taken the corner too sharply, sending it crashing through the sensor gates that lined the parking deck every three feet. There was such a mass of electronics, torn sheet metal, mangled white sensor gates, vines, and concrete rubble from the adjacent column, that he could not see a way through. Sparks shot out over the van from where it had torn through the fat wire couplings that lead into the decontamination chamber.

Burning burning burning burning

With his thumbs tucked into the straps of his backpack, Eli stared at the chamber. The entire time he had been in the building, he had not once dared to go inside. Somehow, even though the support structure and parking deck had at first seemed antagonistic to his presence, the lab had emanated a far stronger feeling that he did not belong inside. Its façade was a constant through each level of the parking deck, almost a background by which he could gain a sense of direction, but never a space that could be occupied. It seemed as if it had never been designed for human habitation, but rather for the hyper-intelligent computers to play out their mathematical equations in search of something beyond the capacity for humans to understand. Now, faced with a sharp sparking heap of metal in front of him and the shorn decking below, he had little choice.

O Lord Thou pluckest me out
O Lord Thou pluckest
burning

004

Phlebas the Phoenician, a fortnight dead,

Eli burst through the doors out onto the roof of the tower, scattering the rocks of a neutered Zen garden. The air tore at his lungs as he raced across the gravel-strewn landscape, throwing bits of dirt and tired brown grass in wide arcs as he went. He slammed bodily into the chest high parapet of the roof, the wind leaving his lungs in great gasps. The edge flexed in minute response to his small frame against its fragile and tormented joints, thick chunks of caulk and unintelligible shards of machinery falling away down the once mobile glass façade of the building. Leaning his upper body dangerously far over the edge, his eyes traced the outlines of circuitry embedded deep within the crystalline confines of the glass panels.

When he had first entered the laboratory, he only felt a mild confusion at its still immaculate interior. None of the vile environments had penetrated the logic of the glass-encrusted tower, and it left Eli with only a vague sense of reality. But as he pressed on, a creeping sensation that he was being watched began to grow steadily in his mind. He felt a cold breath on his neck as he poked about, always looking over his shoulder at the presence that could not be identified. Nearly imperceptible whirring sounds floated through the abandoned conference rooms and frosty offices. Every floor felt the same – quiet, barren, cold and lifeless. He could not be sure, but the glass dividers that were embedded with two-dimensional circuitry seemed to flex and pulse as he had neared each one. He had reached out to touch one to be sure, only to be greeted with a mild static shock and an incredibly cold surface. After passing through a few floors via the fire stairs, the pulsing seemed to grow more intense and the whirring sounds grew louder, eventually being accompanied by the clicking on of compressors and release valves. Eli could only guess that the building was reading his presence and attempting to factor him into its algorithms. The walls sent out indistinct waves of hostility to such a degree that Eli eventually became certain it was trying to delete him from the equation. The terror he would come to feel in the labs was far greater than he had felt in the parking garage.

Even here on the roof he could feel the oppressive weight of the data streams that informed the movement of the structure, overwhelmed by their potential power over his body. Inside, he knew that if he had taken one wrong step he would be consumed by the flexing corners and crushed into the information stream that whirled through every crevice in streaks of bright blue electricity. While he knew his only refuge was to return into the carcass of the deranged support systems, he was not sure he'd be able to handle the six-story descent through the emergency stairwell. It had remained as barren and lifeless as the laboratories had, threatening to clean the life from him in an attempt to maintain its perfectly balanced internal atmosphere. He turned and pushed himself from the edge of the parapet and steeled his nerves for the flight through that inhospitable and entirely inhuman expanse. Clenching his jaw, he forced himself to remember that the adjacent structure would provide him a shelter from this on-slaught of efficiency.

After the frosty silence in the gardens

One foot first, and then the next, Eli began trotting towards the doors from which he had come, eventually breaking into a dead run. The seven data receiving antennae loomed over him like cruel trees covered in tumors. He imagined them sending sweeps of white electrical surges in hard lassos to-wards his feet, ready to bind and hold him here, measured, accounted for, and assimilated into the logic of the hyper-in-telligent laboratory. The doors neared as Eli breathed in short bursts through his mouth. Hands outstretched, he hit the cold steel fire door and yanked it open with all his strength, squinting tightly as he entered and made for the emergency stairs. The brilliantly white hermetic floor seemed to mock him with his own disheveled reflection as he darted across the elevator lobby. Reaching the double door he had left ajar in his ascent, Eli slipped on his torn trousers and went tumbling through the door and down the first flight of stairs; it was as if the building had sensed his apprehension and made him pay for his disrespect. The metallic taste of blood filled his mouth as he tumbled headlong down, thumping his wrist on the handrail and landing heavily upon his left leg. Too terri-fied to nurse his wounds, Eli pulled himself up as quickly as he could and stumbled down the next flight taking as many stairs as he could in leaps. His glance only left his feet to make note of the floor he was passing – 39, 38, 37 and on down to the 34th floor. Nearly missing the door handle, he exploded into the lobby as he heard the faint sound of compressors and gas valves click open. The building was still reading him, noting every movement and drop of sweat that fell from his ruddy face.

We who were living are now dying

With a little patience

Forcing himself from the floor, Eli ran towards the jammed door of the decontamination chamber that would lead towards the melting solace of the support tower beyond. He could almost smell the sweetness of decaying vines beckoning him through as he pushed through small boxes and hanging, damaged sensor gates. Just as Eli emerged through the large gate of the decontamination chamber onto the upper-most deck of the parking structure, he heard them. The three helicopters whirred noisily overhead, casting sweeps of wind and dust at Eli, pushing him sideways along the width of the decking until he collided wetly with the decaying concrete parapet. Its warmth and crumbling grasp comforted him momentarily as he shielded his eyes and attempted to look up. With his left arm stretched across his face, Eli waved frantically with his right, trying to gain the attention of any one of the pilots sent here to douse the structure in a cold chemical death. Focusing on the helicopters above, Eli tottered about the top deck of the parking structure avoiding limp vines and sticky moss where he could manage. He kicked a few pieces over the side and moved towards an external ledge at the periphery of the deck.

Here is no water but only rock

"Please…wait," he mouthed in vain, both hands waving back

and forth, like a marooned refugee of a sunken cruiser. The helicopters seemed not to notice him and waltzed with each other in the sky, looping about with the great diseased building at the center of their dance. Eli stopped waving and merely squinted up at the glinting machines that would not heed his call. He tilted his head slightly and stepped backwards until he felt the edge appear beneath his heel. Eli Warring had no choice at this point, the helicopters ignored him, his colleagues could not reach him, and remaining in the building would surely spell his demise.

A fleeting notion made Eli shake his head once, quickly and violently. With a furrowed brow, he stared across the parking deck towards the gaping hole in the center from which the life-giving machinery was suspended. Only one of the fans on the closest air handler was still functioning, catching itself every now an again on a loose vine that had crept its way into the path of the twirling blade. He considered for a moment that the growth in the support tower had been so thick that it reminded him of a jungle canopy, heavy and dripping, but dense. It had blocked the sun's rays from infiltrating more than a few floors and had clearly shielded the rest of the machinery from the slight rain that had passed while he had been in the laboratory. The deck was wet, but perhaps the interior was still dry.
Dead mountain mouth of carious teeth that cannot spit

'No,' he thought to himself, 'this is insane.' Yet Eli had noticed small patches of undergrowth growing from the ramp that lead down into the cold and dark that housed the server towers. Perhaps out of fear, he had not even considered beginning there when he had arrived. The void that contained the fetid clunking machinery had been so much more enticing, practically pulling him through it in sheer wonder.

He thought of the trunk-like vines at the ground floor and considered it for a moment, still aware of the violent tearing sound the helicopters were making as they adjusted their positions to be sure they would cover every visible square inch.

But dry sterile thunder without rain

'No! What I am thinking? I must be insane. I'd never make it…' Eli berated himself and looked up at the helicopters waving twice more. Nothing. He glanced over his shoulder, causing him to briefly loose his balance. His hands lashed out and grasped a rusted shaft of protruding rebar. Breathing heavily, he watched small pieces of moss alight on the sharp wind that flew up the side of building. He considered he must have been at least two hundred feet off the ground. His body shook involuntarily.

After the agony in stony places

With a loud crack, Eli heard the helicopters gearing up to drop their payload. Small bay doors at the bottom of all three great shimmering bellies opened simultaneously. Without a thought, he found himself running in a dead sprint towards the gaping void not thirty feet in front of him. He made it across the deck in seconds and he leapt up onto the closest air handler, dodging the one operational fan and grasping the supporting column that cleared the top.

Standing fully upright, Eli Warring took a deep breath and hurled himself headlong into the waiting, rotting damp.

A current under sea

Picked his bones in whispers. As he rose and fell

005

Then spoke the thunder

Eli awoke with a start to find himself lying half under a thin white sheet in a cold featureless room. Sitting up, the thin mattress shifted slightly beneath him and he shook his head trying to remember how he had arrived here and where precisely here was. The room was lit by a single circular window of about two feet in diameter that let in a large swath of yellow-grey sunlight. Besides the bed, there was no furniture in the room – the green-grey walls seemed to drip in front of his eyes as they ran uninterrupted all around. As he stood up to walk towards the window, his senses swam from the blood rushing from his head causing him to speculate that he must have been laying down for quite some time. He rubbed his eyes with his palms and walked in the direction of the window. His vision cleared by the time his slow gait brought him to the frame of the window and he looked out on the familiar streetscape of Lexington Avenue far below. His tired eyes followed pedestrians going about their meager daily business until Eli realized he must be in a room at the new Mt. Sinai Psychological Hospital that he had watched rise for the past few months outside his office window. Forgetting the street, his head rang with confusion and alarm just as he heard a quick rapping at the door.

A thin, frail-looking young woman in a pale blue-grey knee-length coat appeared in the doorway, her neck craned low over a clear plastic tablet. "Excuse me, Mr. Sellers, but Dr. Geisel will see you now. He has the results of your evaluation. Please follow me."

My friend, blood shaking my heart

Too bewildered to answer directly, Eli simply nodded and followed the young woman out of the room and down a wide corridor, lit at the far end by another circular porthole – the walls of stainless steel sheathing reflected the light down the hall in diminishing hues of yellow. The young woman tapped at the plastic tablet, upon which small charts flashed, shrank, altered, and calculated in ways Eli was unable to follow in his present state. Every few steps, he would close his eyes to regain some sense of what had happened. His mind raced thinking about his wife and young daughter, his recently deceased father and widowed mother, and his distraught brother on the west coast – surely they knew he was here? Perhaps they were close by. At this thought, he glanced about for a doorway towards what might be a waiting area, but none presented itself. Anxiety mounting, he leaned forward slightly on to the balls of his feet to ask the young woman where his family was. Just as he did so she turned sharply down a hallway to her left and opened a soft plastic door to a rather small office. Saying nothing, she stepped to the side and lifted her hand, palm up, gesturing Eli inside. A rather corpulent man is a light green-grey lab coat, presumably Dr. Geisel, was seated at an immaculately organized desk of the same material of the young woman's tablet. He too was tapping and gesturing intently at the flickering desaturated images embedded in its surface. Eli sniffed the stale air, and the man looked up from his tasks.

"Ah, Eli, good to see you finally looking well." Dr. Geisel said with a quick wrinkled smile and an outstretched hand.

"I – thank you. Doctor, I'm afraid I have no recollection of how I got here or what exactly is going on. If you could be so kind as to start at the beginning and continue slowly, I'd greatly appreciate it," Eli replied after shaking Dr. Geisel's hand and seating himself quickly in front of the desk, eager to be soothed by this medical professional. Somehow he wasn't entirely sure something was amiss, yet his presence in this strange hermetic psychiatric hospital clearly suggested otherwise.

"Ah, that's a shame, but not all that surprising." Dr. Geisel rolled his head to the left and right, rubbing his meaty collarbone with his left hand. Eli shifted forwards in his chair.

"What's a shame? Please, Doctor. What happened?" He felt a prickle at the back of his neck, and his throat tightened. Dr. Geisel sighed heavily.

Only at nightfall, aethereal rumours
"Mr. Sellers, you have been in a coma for quite some time. You were found lying on the subway platform at the 59th and 5th street N station. You were brought here after your wounds had healed, because after an MRI, we detected a sort of resonance patch in the hippocampus region of your brain. This 'patch,' as we've been calling it, has a similar patterning and thickness to others we've found in the surrounding six blocks."

"Others? Other people? I – I'm sorry, I still don't understand."

"You are one of many cases turning up these days. We have discovered survivors – if you can all them that – intermittently for about a month now."

Revive for a moment a broken Coriolanus

"Survivors? Survivors of what?" Eli nearly burst screaming from the room, his knuckles white, gripping the arms of the chair.

"The first few were discovered after they unearthed a portion of diseased concrete that triggered an epileptic reaction in a passer-by, the first of you to make yourselves known. She was completely unaware that she had any relationship to this piece of debris – just imagine the vast amounts of latent information that may be lying dormant within the confines of the subconscious minds of the general populace. It's really quite extraordinary that we can recover the information that we have. After we compiled the positronic brain imaging scans of only a handful of survivors, we can actually reconstruct the space without having a single trace of its construction. There are no remaining photographs or aerial imagery of the structure that we know of and, interestingly, there seems to be a collective amnesia about the entire incident. If it weren't for people such as yourself, that building might as well have not existed at all…" Dr. Geisel trailed off in thought, his forefinger tapping an uneven rhythm on his left cheek. "If there weren't so many of you, I'd venture a hypothesis that it in fact didn't exist."

These fragments I have shored against my ruins

"Doctor, please, what building? What are you talking about?" Eli's brain fought itself in overlapping loops, preventing him from fully comprehending. He was visibly sweating now.
"You were formerly employed by IBM. They sent you into a condemned building to discover why it had become condemned. They lost contact with you about fourteen hours after you entered, and no one had seen you until you were identified on that platform. You disappeared."

With some difficulty, Eli eased himself slowly, painfully back into his chair. Vacantly staring somewhere between his knee and the floor, he could not begin to parse the situation. A slight ringing in his left ear held him motionless – hearing it, he thought nothing but only listened.

London Bridge is falling down falling down falling down

"What these two contradictory images show," Geisel was gesturing at his desk, "is that not only was the building deteriorating from the inside out, but those of you who had taken up some sort of residence in the space were keeping some kind of perverse maintenance alive. Evidence shows that on several occasions, 'residents' would destroy portions to recreate something to their own necessity or liking – a shelter here, a machine shop there, and in one case an accountant's office. That last example was a bit of a blip; some poor soul couldn't handle the psychic trauma as well as you and your peers, and in a way began to revert to his previous life. He used a mix of waste and dead animals to fashion his old office. In a fascinating way he wasn't too far off. A shame nonetheless…"

"This is ridiculous. You're lying. This is total nonsense."

"I like nonsense. It wakes up the brain cells."

Eli looked up. "Didn't Dr. Seuss say that?" Dr. Geisel smiled wanly.
Hieronymo's mad againe.

.....

Originally published on March 20, 2011

12

LABYRINTHS AND OTHER META-PHYSICAL CONSTRUCTIONS: AN INTERVIEW WITH MARC-ANTOINE MATHIEU

Interview with graphic novelist Marc-Antoine Mathieu for MAS Context (Issue 20: Narrative) ///

Léopold Lambert: The specificity of your stories can be found in the subversion of graphic novel's forms and codes. You use its graphic and narrative elements as a creative essence of spatial, temporal and metaphysical labyrinths that compose your books. These labyrinths are not the classical ones, drawn by a demiurge architect from above, who is laughing to see all these small bodies getting lost in the complexity of his lines. The labyrinths you create seem to me in the continuity of another form, invented by Franz Kafka, where the author is also lost within the labyrinths he created. Not only his stories are labyrinthine but so is the medium: at Kafka's death, *The Trial* (1925) was a disarticulated sum of chapters that his friend, Max Brod, reconstituted retrospectively – and erroneously, in my opinion – to give them a logical order. Similarly, *The Castle* (1926) ends in the middle of a sentence… How important is the figure of the labyrinth for you?

Marc-Antoine Mathieu: The labyrinth is indeed a form

that has been working on me for quite a while. It has been a while indeed since you don't "enter" the labyrinth just like that. It's a bit like the color, or the absolute. There are many things that we hesitate to enter; we have to think twice first. The next book that I am going to publish in October will be called *Labyrinthum* [L'Association Publisher] and it will be a fractal labyrinth. It will be fractal since, for me, the labyrinth is more Borgesian than Kafkaesque. I would say that what is Kafkaesque is a literature of the absurd, whereas Borges is more a poetry of metaphysics. I think that the labyrinth is more a metaphysical figure than an absurd figure.

At least in my work, this is true, the labyrinth is always somewhere. Perhaps it is an illusion, though. I mean that it might not be the 'true' labyrinth in the sense of a complete loss of references in something that we built for ourselves. I don't think that this is the labyrinth that I am talking about. The interesting thing with the labyrinth is indeed the experience of losing our references; it means the experience of losing ourselves, the loss of our own reality, or so-called reality. This way, it is true that there is the artist's symbolic in the labyrinth, because what is the artist doing if he or she is not trying to lose himself or herself in his or her creation in order to experiment always further? There is a risk of madness in the labyrinth, and this is why that we don't enter it immediately. It is a figure of maturity or, on the other hand, a figure of survival: this is Ulysses who is obliged to go through the labyrinth. Either he dies in it or he survives it. My next story will have for only setting only a labyrinthine route, in the Borgesian sense, that is the desert-labyrinth.

Léopold Lambert: You are referring to Borges's short story, *The Two Kings and the Two Labyrinths* [1939], aren't you? You seem to be indeed more interested in Borges's labyrinth than in James Joyce's labyrinth, since that is what is implicit in this

story: Joyce creates literary labyrinths full of complex apparatuses, and Borges, on the contrary, produce labyrinths in the
form of deserts. We find a lot of those in your work.

Marc-Antoine Mathieu: Yes, it is an infinite erratic labyrinth
that ignores its own status. In my next book, there is a character who is lost in the desert but who does not know that he
is in a labyrinth. This is a type of awareness we can call the
awareness of the demiurge. The form of the labyrinth is here
but it is not represented. It is a roving that goes to the right,
to the left, straight ahead, that gets lost, but there are neither
walls nor structures: there is no architecture.

One can find the labyrinth in most of my stories. There is also
the labyrinthine story, the fact that it can be cyclical or in the
form of a spiral. Another labyrinth, just as pure as the desert
is the spiral. In a spiral, wherever you are, you are simultaneously in the center and at the periphery. It is almost the
symbol of the labyrinth. The most radical form of the labyrinth
makes us wonder if we are on the wall or between the walls.
In a spiral, whether you are on a spire or between two spires,
it is the same thing at the end of the day: you are on something that eludes your understanding. In a certain way, you
are trapped. That might be where the labyrinth can join the
figure of the absurd in the sense of Albert Camus.

Léopold Lambert: The 'Sisyphean' absurd.

Marc-Antoine Mathieu: That's it.

Léopold Lambert: We can observe several layers or levels
of architecture in your books. There is architecture in a rela-
tively classical sense, as you use it in your story, far from neu-
tral: the various City departments' architecture for example,
the Station in La Qu... [Delcourt, 1991], but also the giant

computer in *Dead Memory* [Dark Horse, 2004]. There is also the architecture of the book page, with which you play (empty frame, anti-frame, the page in the page in the page, etc.) and the architecture of the book itself, as an object that involves both the author and the reader inside the narrative. How do you articulate these various levels of architecture?

Marc-Antoine Mathieu: I prefer to leave this analysis to specialists. Personally I am not so interested in doing it. That being said, what I would be interested in doing, is to elaborate on the fact that I am thinking of myself more as an architect than a story teller. I feel that I am more a space and time manager than a narrator. I have the feeling that, often, the narrative, the dialogues, the texts are pretexts to set up a space-time of which I am less in control. It is as if with words, with dialogues, with a story, I was building a skeleton and what is really interesting is everything that happens around this skeleton that I build from book to book. Each time I am adding some flesh to the skeleton and this flesh belongs much more to the world of architecture – sometimes, even a scientific architecture – than to the world of literature. That is what might make the specificity of my work.

Your question can be pertinent to the extent that the distinctions between some arts can be interesting. When I created *3 secondes* [Delcourt, 2011], for example, I did not feel that I was producing a graphic novel at all. I was feeling much more that I was in an architect's shoes, someone that had made a sketch of a bridge, and that, later, had to wonder about engineering problems for six months, wondering how this can hold itself, which pathway I should add to it, which spring to adjust so that it can work and that the whole thing would be quite harmonious. I was wondering much more about structural questions than narrative ones. Structure is a notion of space and time; much more than narrative that

JE COMMIS L'ERREUR DE VOULOIR RATTRAPER LE PROMENEUR. IL ME DISTANÇA TRÈS VITE, CAR PLUS EXERCÉ QUE MOI À MARCHER SUR LES MURETS. BIENTÔT JE NE LE VIS PLUS ET LORSQUE JE VOULUS REBROUSSER CHEMIN POUR RETROUVER MON APPARTEMENT, JE DUS ME RENDRE À L'ÉVIDENCE : JE M'ÉTAIS PERDU.

calls for concept like linearity, for example. Linearity is what is appearing: there is a dialogue, it is fluid, it seems quite obvious. In *Le décalage* [Delcourt, 2013], the dialogues are following one another, they look similar and we seem to surf on a sort of a crest, but actually, what is weaved around it is something completely different, something that escapes from me completely. I don't know how to analyze it. That is what is interesting by the way. What eludes me at this specific moment, it can only escape from me this way, only in this medium that we call graphic novel. It is a sort of mix between a shaping of time, a shaping of space, convergence lines, a sort of alchemy that not only I am not interested in analyzing but I actually refuse to do so, as it is my terrain of adventures and experiments.

Léopold Lambert: That is perfect, since I wanted to ask you a question about graphic novel as a specific medium and you just answered it.

Marc-Antoine Mathieu: The specificity of graphic novel, lies in what it makes of the drawing. It creates shapes/forms but without designating them completely. Cinema, on the contrary, produces forms but automatically designates them. In a graphic novel, you can draw shapes/forms without designating them, by giving them masks. That is what I do in my books: The City Department of Justice, the City Department of Humor, whatever Palace, the Station, etc. They are things that I designate, but only partially, 10% or 35% of it, or that I even de-designate, I non-designate them. It creates shapes/forms but they are shapes that the reader will have to complete. The reader is the one who has to designate them completely. That is the challenge.

There is also space-time. Time is the same thing: we designate a time but what is it? Will the reading of the book take five minutes? Half an hour? Three hours? This time that is defined by the graphic novel is very blurry and mysterious. We can even go backwards… There is also some text. We think that we dominate it but if we work on it a bit, we can leave blurs, holes, ellipses, shortcuts, it can go very far. Graphic novel is a true terrain of experiments, somewhere between genres and mediation tools that make an unoccupied lot (terrain vague), where anyone can have fun experimenting as a creator and experimenting the way the reader reads.

Léopold Lambert: If I follow you, the graphic novel is also an object, and you have been playing with this object over time. If I just evoke the covers themselves, *L'épaisseur du miroir* [Delcourt, 1995] has two covers and two reading directions, *Le décalage* [Delcourt, 2013] has an order of pages that seemed to have shifted in such a way that the story starts on the cover and what should have been the cover can be only found at the end of the book. There are multiple other similar examples.

Marc-Antoine Mathieu: Yes, we can play with the fourth dimension or an analogy of the fourth dimension when we start to consider that the graphic novel is indeed an object, an image book that I have in my hands as a reader. When I find a spiral that seems to exit the book, a pop-up, color or a torn page, I am starting to ask myself some questions.

Léopold Lambert: It is interesting that you speak of a fourth dimension. For us, readers, the book is the third dimension, but for your characters that it is a fourth dimension, isn't it? What is our own fourth dimension? Is there a great object in which we can also be read in one way or another?

Marc-Antoine Mathieu: That's it. It was the idea of *L'origine* [Delcourt, 1990], the first book of Julius : to create a kind

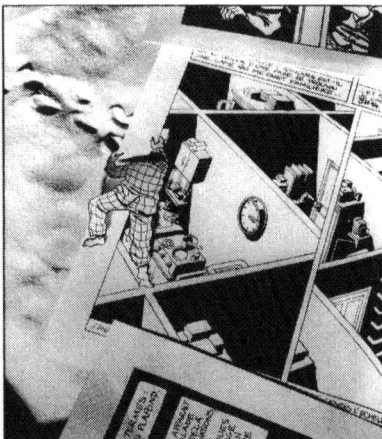

DESTIN OU FATALITÉ ? TOUJOURS EST-IL QU'AU DÉTOUR D'UNE PAGE, JE TROUVAI UNE CASE QUI ME PARUT FAMILIÈRE...

...ET POUR CAUSE : JE RECONNUS MON APPARTEMENT ; CELUI QUE JE CHERCHAIS ; C'ÉTAIT BIEN LUI, AVEC SA PENDULE QUI INDIQUAIT 3H14, L'HEURE EXACTE À LAQUELLE JE L'AVAIS QUITTÉ.

J'AVAIS ENFIN RETROUVÉ MON RÊVE !

...JE DESCENDIS L'ÉCHELLE MURALE...

...ET ME RECOUCHAI...

of vertigo, an existential story within the story. If these two-dimensional characters were becoming aware that they were living in a world that had actually three dimensions, then we could also try to imagine that there is a fourth dimension. When we listen to astrophysicists nowadays, that is what they attempt to explain to us: try to imagine that time is also a dimension, I mean a physical dimension and you will have a richer and more complete image of the universe in which we live. Einstein is the one who updated all that: he looked under the carpet and he discovered that the three Newtonian dimensions could not explain everything. It remains, however, very hard to imagine. A four-dimensional world is not something intuitive. The space-time light cone is very hard to imagine, even with a lot of imagination. Sometimes, we succeed imperfectly to have a glance at what it is, but it so complicated. That might be where the artist can help.

Let's go back to *L'origine* and this analogy of a two-dimensional world that lives on a sphere. In this two-dimensional world, characters and scientists discover that their world is a gigantic sphere and that if they go in one direction, they will ultimately go back to their starting point. Other characters, obviously, wonder what this madness is all about, what this sphere means. They are in two dimensions, it is not possible; there is no thickness. They are being told that they have to imagine that there is a third dimension. The scientists are being called crazy, but at the end of the day, it is our own situation as well: we are prisoners of a three-dimensional world and of the illusion of the world in which we are embedded. Yet, the fourth dimension exists, we have to deal with it.

Léopold Lambert: In *Dead Memory*, a multitude of walls grows overnight in an endless city. These walls are blocking the streets that become different spaces. In order to move, some squads of miners/policemen go through the houses' walls. This has very poignant historical references. There is Auguste Blanqui and the 19th-century Parisian revolutions, there is the Israeli army that went through the walls and Palestinian living rooms during the 2002 siege on Nablus's refugee camp. We can also evoke the fictitious opening scene of Terry Gilliam's *Brazil,* where a character is arrested by policemen who swarm inside his apartment from the ceiling. Can you tell us about your interpretation of architecture as a material assemblage and its political consequences?

Marc-Antoine Mathieu: I have an interest in history, but what interests me in *Dead Memory,* is to lift my antennas and to express in the best way as possible, the feelings, intuitions, instinctive thoughts that I can have about the polis, the city, new networks that are being created, etc. I did *Dead Memory* fifteen years ago now, but from what I heard, it might have pointed out a few things. Walls that are interacting and emerging with the city are a bit the symbol of a society that would like to declare itself transparent, open to everything, but that actually closes itself to everything. I formalized it through these walls in quite a radical manner. I would say that it is not the best of my books, since it is a bit rigid, a bit stuck, and talkative, even. The sociological domain is not the field where I feel the most comfortable.

.....

Originally published on December 17, 2013
(also published as a podcast on Archipelago)

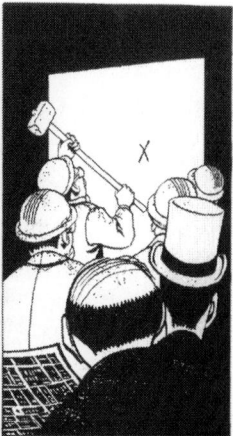

13

OVERPOPULATED CITIES / THE CONCENTRATION CITY, BILLENNIUM, L'ORIGINE & SOYLENT GREEN

This chapter offers a short inventory of four worlds with over-populated cities, thus embodying an extreme vision of cities that already exist. These four worlds are depicted in two short stories, *The Concentration City* and *Billennium* by James Graham Ballard, in the graphic novel *L'Origine* by Marc-Antoine Mathieu and in the film *Soylent Green* directed by Richard Felischer.

Ballard's two short stories, *The Concentration City* (1957) and *Billennium* (1962) describe two situations that could actually belong to the same world. While the first one depicts an infinite dense city in which 'free space' and 'non-functional space' are considered as an oxymoron and impossible to fathom, the second describes a urban code that forbids anybody to live in more than 3.5 square meters (38 sq ft). In *The Concentration City*, the main character travels East on a train looking for free space that would allow him to test his flying invention and realized after several days spent on this train that he came back to his departure point both in space (coming from the West) and in time (the day he came back is the same day that he left). In *Billenium* the two protagonists finds a few extra square meters hidden behind a wall that they use as a clandestine shelter before realizing that they re-created the same density that they were originally running away from.

Those two short stories might have inspired graphic novel author Marc-Antoine Mathieu in his invention of incredible Kafkaesque worlds whose philosophical dimension is the systematic questioning of the media they exist in (the graphic novel itself). In *L'Origine* (1990), Mathieu depicts a city where the streets are so densely populated that the skills to extract yourself from the crowd to reach the building you would like to enter are recognized as a daily need for survival.

In an evocative scene, two characters appear to live in a suprisingly spacious apartment. Suddenly, they stop their discussion and run to push every piece of furniture to the side and open the wood floor before standing themselves on the edge of the void, as next page reveals that their apartment is actually in the middle of the elevator shaft. The caption reads that they have to accomplish this radical 'ceremonial' up to sixty times a day. Through it, we can recall the market in Bangkok that needs to make room a few times a day for the train that passes right through it.

The last example for this chapter is in Richard Fleisher's *Soylent Green* (1973), where millions of people living in the proletarian district (separated by a wall from the bourgeois district) sleep in churches, cars and staircases. The agora is overcrowded as well and when a demonstration is about to start, the police uses bulldozers to arrest people considering the dense mass of bodies as a unique material to evacuate. The government offers euthanasia to people, who desire to die. Before receiving a lethal injection, the volunteers can watch a short movie of the world as it existed before overcrowding, giving them one last pleasant experience before they die. What the main character discovers, however, is that

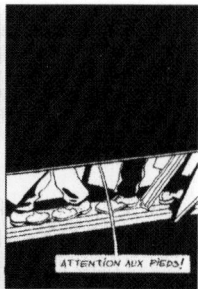

the cadavers are then brought to a gigantic factory where they are transformed into food that is given to the proletariat, the "soylent green" that gives the title to the movie.

Illustrations are screenshots of Soylent Green by Richard Fleisher (1973) and excerpt of *L'Origine* by Marc-Antoine Mathieu (Delcourt, 1990).

.....

Originally published on June 12, 2012

14

FAHRENHEIT 451 BY RAY BRADBURY

The two excerpts from Ray Bradbury's *Fahrenheit 451* (1953) describe the systematic destruction of books accomplished by firemen, understood here as men who burn books. Books have been banned for their ability to describe another world, and therefore, their invitation to embrace subversive (dis)orders. When Bradbury writes his book in 1953, the Nazi *auto-dafés* (etymologically act of faith, used to describe public executions during the Spanish Inquisition before it was applied to book burning ceremonies) still belong to a close history. In our own recent history, the Koran has been burnt twice, with a disturbing media coverage. In Rabah Ameur-Zaïmeche's new historical film, *Les Chants de Mandrin* (Smugglers' Songs) set in 18th-century France, the police burns the contraband manifesto that smugglers attempt to spread and that was printed clandestinely – the philosopher Jean-Luc Nancy plays the role of the pirate printer.

Books are poetic objects. Embodied by paper, they carry their own fragility and constitute their own combustible when a power decides to annihilate them. Books are the medium through which ideas acquire a virtual eternity and for this reason deserve to be passionately salvaged. But this eternity is only virtual, because a small sparkle can inflame them and destroy them forever.

FAHRENHEIT 451 (excerpts) ///
By Ray Bradbury (New York: Ballantine Books, 1953)

IT WAS A PLEASURE TO BURN

IT was a special pleasure to see things eaten, to see things blackened and changed. With the brass nozzle in his fists, with this great python spitting its venomous kerosene upon the world, the blood pounded in his head, and his hands were the hands of some amazing conductor playing all the symphonies of blazing and burning to bring down the tatters and charcoal ruins of history. With his symbolic helmet numbered 451 on his stolid head, and his eyes all orange flame with the thought of what came next, he flicked the igniter and the house jumped up in a gorging fire that burned the evening sky red and yellow and black. He strode in a swarm of fireflies. He wanted above all, like the old joke, to shove a marshmallow on a stick in the furnace, while the flapping pigeon-winged books died on the porch and lawn of the house. While the books went up in sparkling whirls and blew away on a wind turned dark with burning.

—-

Montag's hand closed like a mouth, crushed the book with wild devotion, with an insanity of mindlessness to his chest. The men above were hurling shovelfuls of magazines into the dusty air. They fell like slaughtered birds and the woman stood below, like a small girl, among the bodies.
Montag had done nothing. His hand had done it all, his hand, with a brain of its own, with a conscience and a curiosity in each trembling finger, had turned thief.. Now, it plunged the book back under his arm, pressed it tight to sweating armpit, rushed out empty, with a magician's flourish! Look here! Innocent! Look!

He gazed, shaken, at that white hand. He held it way out, as if he were far-sighted. He held it close, as if he were blind.

"Montag! "

He jerked about.

"Don't stand there, idiot!"

The books lay like great mounds of fishes left to dry. The men danced and slipped and fell over them. Titles glittered their golden eyes, falling, gone.

"Kerosene! They pumped the cold fluid from the numbered 451 tanks strapped to their shoulders. They coated each book, they pumped rooms full of it.

They hurried downstairs, Montag staggered after them in the kerosene fumes.

"Come on, woman!"

The woman knelt among the books, touching the drenched leather and cardboard, reading the gilt titles with her fingers while her eyes accused Montag.

"You can't ever have my books," she said.

"You know the law," said Beatty. "Where's your common sense? None of those books agree with each other. You've been locked up here for years with a regular damned Tower of Babel. Snap out of it! The people in those books never lived. Come on now! "

She shook her head.

"The whole house is going up;" said Beatty,

The men walked clumsily to the door. They glanced back at Montag, who stood near the woman.

"You're not leaving her here?" he protested.

"She won't come."

"Force her, then!"

Beatty raised his hand in which was concealed the igniter. "We're due back at the house. Besides, these fanatics always try suicide; the pattern's familiar."

Montag placed his hand on the woman's elbow. "You can come with me."

"No," she said. "Thank you, anyway."

"I'm counting to ten," said Beatty. "One. Two."

"Please," said Montag.

"Go on," said the woman.

"Three. Four."

"Here." Montag pulled at the woman.

The woman replied quietly, "I want to stay here"

"Five. Six."

"You can stop counting," she said. She opened the fingers of one hand slightly and in the palm of the hand was a single slender object.

An ordinary kitchen match.

The sight of it rushed the men out and down away from the house. Captain Beatty, keeping his dignity, backed slowly through the front door, his pink face burnt and shiny from a thousand fires and night excitements. God, thought Montag, how true! Always at night the alarm comes. Never by day! Is it because the fire is prettier by night?

.....

Originally published on March 21, 2012

15

NEVER LET ME GO
BY MARK ROMANEK

Never Let Me Go is a 2010 film directed by Mark Romanek and adapted from the novel by Kazuo Ishiguro.

We could distinguish two types of successful science-fiction films: those that visually invent a world either speculative or metaphorical, which strike us for its inventivity; and the others that do not allow any kind of special effects, and introduce a plot directly within a recognizable world that moves us because of our proximity to that depicted society. *Never Let Me Go* is in this latter category.

The film starts in the 1970s, in a country boarding school isolated from the world. Classes and the general atmosphere is similar to what we know of boarding schools at this time, except that we later understand that all students are destined to become organ donors until they "complete" (die) following their donations. The story thus follows three of these children in their youth, experiencing love and friendship just like any other human beings.

These "other human beings" are actually rarely present in this movie, and one could see in this, the loss of humanity in those who created. These un-humans end up being the only representatives of humanity.

This film illustrates the institutionalization of the production of exclusion in which Michel Foucault was eminently interested and that he investigated in several of his books such as *The Birth of the Clinic* (1963) and *The History of Sexuality* (1976). In this case, the exclusion is even more vicious, as it is re-included within the system in an absolute scheme of exploitation from one category to another. It is interesting to see that the same exploitation is integrated and accepted thanks to a shift of terminology. Donors do not die, they "complete" and they are said to "donate" their organs as if they actually chose it. Of course, the fact that this society does not necessarily imply a new architecture seems to be less interesting for architects; however this shift of terminology interests us as citizens as this occur on a daily basis in our current society; also, one should be careful about the way architecture is dealt with in this film. It is very subtle, but from the heterotopic Victorian Boarding School to the austere post-modern concrete hospital via the typical English coastal houses reproduced several time along the street, without being inherently linked to this specific system, carry appropriately the dehumanized space of this society.

.....

Originally published on March 14, 2011

16

THE DECLAMATORY
PORCELAIN ARCHITECTURES
OF SERGE BRUSSOLO

Serge Brussolo is a French science-fiction writer whose best novels and short stories written in the 1980s. In this regard, the story of *Aussi lourd que le vent* (As Heavy as the Wind) narrates the invention of a new form of art (and by exension, architecture) that introduces voice's frequencies as a means of materialization of evanescent porcelain volumes. Brussolo goes as far as suggesting a sort of counter-Kaballah as the words screamed by the artist that seem to produce the most beautiful pieces are insults.

When they disapear, these porcelain volumes release the sound that generated them just as if their materiality were strictly composed by sound itself that could transform itself from waves to solid and back to waves again. At the end of the narrative, a venal patron manages to make the volume permanent and sell it to the building industry that produces entire buildings in this unbreakable porcelain.

With this story, Brussolo invented a new way of creating architecture: a declamatory design that requires the architect to recite or improvise a composition of sounds and words that materialize into porcelain. It also celebrates the creation of architecture as a ceremony that owes something to the

Kaballah, the Judaic quest of God through mathematics of the words that describe God. The mythical Golem whose life comes from the power of the words is here not activated by the word of god but, rather, by insults. I would like to think of this as an homage to Antonin Artaud.

AUSSI LOURD QUE LE VENT (excerpts) ///
By Serge Brussolo (my translation)

" She screamed :
" Earth ! "
She felt the air ringing from her teeth with an extraordinary violence and on a frequency close to ultrasound and probably inaudible. The name was already materializing itself between the drifting wisps of mist in the form of an imperfect sphere, made out of a milky white and that was softly rolling along the sandy slope. Nel got on her knees, her hands stretched to receive against her stomach, the solidification of the word pronounced a few seconds earlier. It was a mass as big as a soup tureen both soft and resistant, whose brightness recalled Chinese porcelain. A kind of monster born from the coupling of a giant teacup and a Ming vase. All over the surface run a thin network of cracks similar to blood vessels under a too thin skin.

" No," she forced herself to think, "they are objects. Only objects."

There was enough here to establish the basis of a new art: the vocal sculpture, the sung mold, the poem bas-relief, and sometimes she was shivering when she tought of the commercial aspects of such a discovery! Wouldn't developers, architects be tempted to create houses by voice? To build entire cities with only manpower, a well trained choir, a box of solution and a needle? She pictured immaculate cities rising, extracted from the nil by a lament, a recitative carefully designed on an architect's drafting table or on any crooked developer's desk. Fortunately, the very evanescence of the production, the ephemeral aspect of forms created by sound or clamor, was protecting them from any commercial speculation. The scream-sculpture will remain within the domain of art, and no contractor will ever use them to make money. The work's fragility was becoming its best defense, and the brevity of its life was its best guarantee of eternity.

"The sun was lighting its first reflections on the high creamy and bluish barrier of projects which was occupying the Southern part of the city's horizon. A thousand housing units born from nothingness during only three nights. Products of a strange technology that Rene was not really sure he understood. Projects born from the song intoned by a choir of architects-baritones who were operating only at night. They were raising, in the middle of darkness, those buildings supported by soft and bright walls like porcelain and yet surprisingly resistant. […]

Although Rene was remembering having read in a dissident newspaper an article about a day-time catastrophe in which a thirty stories tower suddenly disappeared as if by magic, abandoning its tenants in the void with their furniture, their televisions. Letting them collapse on the asphalt in a horrible pile of wrecked bodies."

.....

Originally published on June 4, 2011

ABOUT

THE FUNAMBULIST: a blog written and edited by Léopold Lambert. It finds its name in the consideration for architecture's representative medium, the line, and its philosophical and political power when it materializes and subjectivizes bodies. If the white page represents a given milieu — a desert, for example — and one (an architect, for example) comes to trace a line on it, (s)he will virtually split this same milieu into two distinct impermeable parts through its embodiment, the wall. The Funambulist, also known as a tightrope walker, is the character who, somehow, subverts this power by walking on the line.

CENTER FOR TRANSFORMATIVE MEDIA, Parsons The New School for Design: a transdisciplinary media research initiative bridging design and the social sciences, and dedicated to the exploration of the transformative potential of emerging technologies upon the foundational practices of everyday life across a range of settings.

PUNCTUM BOOKS: spontaneous acts of scholarly combustion is an open-access and print-on-demand independent publisher dedicated to radically creative modes of intellectual inquiry and writing across a whimsical para-humanities assemblage. punctum books seeks to curate the open spaces of writing or writing-as-opening, the crucial tiny portals on whose capacious thresholds all writing properly and improperly takes place. Pricking, puncturing, perforating = publishing in the mode of an unconditional hospitality and friendship, making space for what Eve Sedgwick called "queer little gods" – the "ontologically intermediate and teratological figures" of y/our thought. We seek to pierce and disturb the wednesdayish, business-as-usual protocols of both the generic university studium and its individual cells or holding tanks. We also take in strays.

12950958R00061

Printed in Great Britain
by Amazon.co.uk, Ltd.,
Marston Gate.